D0948442

✫✫✫✫✫✫✫✫✫✫✫✫✫✫✫✫✫

BASEBALL
SUPERSTARS

Rickey Henderson

✫✫✫✫✫✫✫✫✫✫✫✫✫✫✫✫✫

✷✷✷✷✷✷✷✷✷✷✷✷✷✷✷✷✷

Hank Aaron
Ty Cobb
Johnny Damon
Lou Gehrig
Rickey Henderson
Derek Jeter
Randy Johnson   Mike Piazza
Andruw Jones   Kirby Puckett
Mickey Mantle   Albert Pujols
Roger Maris   Mariano Rivera
                         Jackie Robinson
                         Babe Ruth
                         Curt Schilling
                         Ichiro Suzuki
                         Bernie Williams
                         Ted Williams

✷✷✷✷✷✷✷✷✷✷✷✷✷✷✷✷✷

✦ ✦ ✦ ✦ ✦ ✦ ✦ ✦ ✦ ✦ ✦ ✦ ✦ ✦ ✦

BASEBALL SUPERSTARS

Rickey Henderson

Greg Roensch

CHELSEA HOUSE
PUBLISHERS
An imprint of Infobase Publishing

✦ ✦ ✦ ✦ ✦ ✦ ✦ ✦ ✦ ✦ ✦ ✦ ✦ ✦ ✦

RICKEY HENDERSON
Copyright © 2008 by Infobase Publishing

Chelsea House
An imprint of Infobase Publishing
132 West 31st Street
New York NY 10001

Library of Congress Cataloging-in-Publication Data

Roensch, Greg.
  Rickey Henderson / Greg Roensch.
    p. cm. — (Baseball superstars)
  Includes bibliographical references and index.
  ISBN 978-0-7910-9601-7 (hardcover)
  1. Henderson, Rickey, 1958– 2. Baseball players—United States—Biography. 3. African
American baseball players—Biography. I. Title. II. Series.
  GV865.H46R64 2008
  796.357092--dc22
  [B]   2007029051

Chelsea House books are available at special discounts when purchased in bulk quantities
for businesses, associations, institutions, or sales promotions. Please call our Special Sales
Department in New York at (212) 967-8800 or (800) 322-8755.

You can find Chelsea House on the World Wide Web at http://www.chelseahouse.com

Series design by Erik Lindstrom
Cover design by Ben Peterson

Printed in the United States of America

Bang EJB 10 9 8 7 6 5 4 3 2 1

This book is printed on acid-free paper.

All links and Web addresses were checked and verified to be correct at the time
of publication. Because of the dynamic nature of the Web, some addresses and links
may have changed since publication and may no longer be valid.

✳ ✳ ✳ ✳ ✳ ✳ ✳ ✳ ✳ ✳ ✳ ✳ ✳ ✳ ✳ ✳ ✳

CONTENTS

A Superstar
with Style

On October 17, 1989, the Oakland Athletics and the San Francisco Giants were getting ready to face each other in the third game of the World Series. Both teams were coming off impressive victories in their respective League Championship Series, but the Giants were now in big trouble. After losing the first two World Series games in Oakland, the Giants badly needed to turn the tide at their home stadium, Candlestick Park. Unfortunately for the Giants, the A's looked unbeatable. They were a great team, and they were playing very well. In addition, Oakland seemed to have extra motivation to win because it had lost the World Series the previous year. As fans filed into the ballpark and the players made their final pre-game preparations, Candlestick Park was buzzing with excitement. Then, about a half-hour before the first pitch, a huge

An earthquake measuring 7.1 on the Richter Scale struck the San Francisco Bay Area on October 17, 1989, about a half-hour before the start of Game 3 of the World Series between the Oakland A's and the San Francisco Giants. Here, the crowd at Candlestick Park waits to hear if the game will be played or not. The game would be canceled, and the World Series would resume 10 days later.

earthquake rocked the stadium and the San Francisco Bay area. It only lasted for 15 seconds, but those 15 seconds seemed like an eternity.

Before the quake, the people of San Francisco, Oakland, and the rest of the region had been filled with a tremendous amount of enthusiasm over this first-ever World Series meeting between the two Bay Area teams. All of that fervor changed, however, when the earthquake hit. In the blink of an eye, everyone's attention shifted from the game of baseball to the death and destruction caused by the massive tremor, which killed 62 people and left more than 12,000 others homeless in Northern California. In the moments and hours after the quake, it was hard for anyone to imagine playing or watching a baseball game, even if it was the World Series. There was talk of moving the remaining games to another part of California or maybe even canceling the World Series altogether.

When play resumed after a 10-day break, the A's went on to sweep the Giants to become champions of the "Earthquake Series." It was not a huge surprise that the A's won the 1989 World Series. The talented team was loaded with a mighty lineup and a great pitching staff, and the A's were very motivated after the previous year's loss. In fact, many experts had picked Oakland to win it all even before the start of the season. Still, the A's did not find it easy to win in 1989. They had to overcome injuries to key players throughout the season. Fortunately, the team was good enough and deep enough to win in spite of the injuries.

The A's also benefited from a bold midseason trade that further boosted the team's chances for success. On June 21, 1989, the A's acquired leadoff man extraordinaire Rickey Henderson from the New York Yankees. Henderson fit in with the team immediately and provided the spark at the top of the batting order that helped the A's win 99 games during the season, the most wins of any team that year. As good as Henderson was during the regular season, he elevated his game even more in the postseason to lead the A's to World Series glory, batting .400 in the American League Championship Series and .474 in the World Series.

A HALL OF FAME CAREER

When the A's acquired Henderson for their play-off push in 1989, it was his second stint with the team. He first played in

In the first inning of the first game of the 1989 American League Championship Series, Rickey Henderson of the Oakland A's stole second base. Toronto second baseman Nelson Liriano was covering the bag. Henderson, whom the A's acquired in midseason, was named the MVP of the championship series.

Oakland from 1979 to 1984, before being traded to the Yankees prior to the 1985 season. By the time Henderson rejoined the A's, he was firmly established as baseball's premier leadoff man and one of the game's most exciting and productive players. In fact, the A's reacquired Henderson at the peak of his career. His play in the 1989 postseason earned him the Most Valuable Player award for the American League Championship Series. The following year, he went on to score a bigger prize—MVP of the American League. His statistics during that stellar season: a .325 batting average, 119 runs scored, 97 walks, 65 steals in 75 attempts, and 159 hits including 28 home runs.

Those two awards are just a couple of the highlights in Henderson's long career. Although he has not played in the major leagues since 2003, Henderson has not officially announced his retirement. It is becoming increasingly likely, though, that he will not play in the majors again. If he does not play again, he will be eligible for the Baseball Hall of Fame in 2009 (players can be voted into the Hall of Fame after five years have passed since their last major-league game). Looking at the following list of career highlights, it is clear that Henderson should be elected to the Hall of Fame just as soon as he becomes eligible. Here are some of Henderson's achievements:

- Henderson played for nine Major League Baseball teams during his 25-year career. He was on the Oakland A's four times for a total of 14 years. He also played for the New York Yankees, the Toronto Blue Jays, the San Diego Padres (twice), the Anaheim Angels, the New York Mets, the Seattle Mariners, the Boston Red Sox, and the Los Angeles Dodgers.
- He was an All-Star 10 times in his first 13 seasons.
- In addition to the win with the 1989 Athletics, Henderson also won a second World Series with the Toronto Blue Jays in 1993.
- Besides winning the American League MVP award in 1990, he finished in the top three in MVP voting on two other occasions.
- He hit 297 home runs, including a major-league-record 81 homers to lead off a game.
- He became the twenty-fifth player in baseball history to join the 3,000-hit club.
- He broke Babe Ruth's all-time record for most walks in a career, with 2,190. Henderson was subsequently passed by Barry Bonds.

- Henderson broke Ty Cobb's career record for most runs scored. His record stands at 2,295.

As these achievements indicate, Henderson deserves to be mentioned in the same breath with some of the game's most elite players. Yet, he will be remembered for one aspect of his game more than any other. Henderson will go down in history as the greatest base stealer—by far—to ever play the game. In 1980, his first full season in the majors, Henderson became the first American League player and only the third player in

★ ★ ★ ★ ☆

THE ART OF STEALING

It certainly helps to be fast to be a great base stealer. Speed, however, is not the only requirement. Here are a few other factors that go into making a successful stolen-base artist:

- **TAKE A GOOD LEAD.** The larger a base runner's lead, the closer he is to his destination. The perfect lead is one in which the runner is just far enough off the bag that he could barely get back safely if the pitcher tried to pick him off.
- **READ THE PITCHER.** Every pitcher has a different pickoff move. A good base stealer knows how to read the pitcher's motion to tell if he is going to throw to the plate or try to nail the runner with a pickoff move.
- **GET A GOOD JUMP.** Once a base runner decides to run, he must take off as soon as he is sure the pitcher is delivering the ball to the plate. It takes full commitment to steal a base, but the timing has to be perfect. If a runner leaves too early, he will be picked off. On the other hand, if he hesitates, he will be thrown out by the catcher.

baseball history to steal 100 bases in a season. He went on to accomplish this feat two more times, including in 1982, when he stole an incredible 130 bases to break Lou Brock's single-season record. In 1991, Henderson again ran past Brock into the record books when he stole his 939th base to become the all-time stolen-base king. Henderson's amazing record stands at 1,406 steals. It is often said that records were made to be broken; it's hard to imagine anyone ever coming close to this one.

Besides all of his records and accomplishments, Henderson will be remembered for his unique personality on the baseball

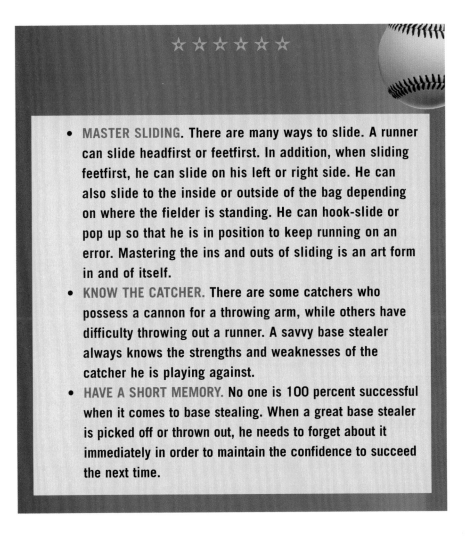

☆ ☆ ☆ ☆ ☆

- **MASTER SLIDING. There are many ways to slide. A runner can slide headfirst or feetfirst. In addition, when sliding feetfirst, he can slide on his left or right side. He can also slide to the inside or outside of the bag depending on where the fielder is standing. He can hook-slide or pop up so that he is in position to keep running on an error. Mastering the ins and outs of sliding is an art form in and of itself.**
- **KNOW THE CATCHER. There are some catchers who possess a cannon for a throwing arm, while others have difficulty throwing out a runner. A savvy base stealer always knows the strengths and weaknesses of the catcher he is playing against.**
- **HAVE A SHORT MEMORY. No one is 100 percent successful when it comes to base stealing. When a great base stealer is picked off or thrown out, he needs to forget about it immediately in order to maintain the confidence to succeed the next time.**

Among Rickey Henderson's many skills, his greatest was his prowess as a base stealer. Here, on May 1, 1991, he celebrated the 939th stolen base of his career, which broke Lou Brock's major-league record. Henderson went on to record nearly 500 more stolen bases.

field. He definitely had a style all his own, from his exciting headfirst slides and signature one-handed snatch catches to the way he talked to himself in the batter's box and carried on conversations with fans while standing in the outfield.

Henderson's critics complained that he was a showboat, or a hot dog. In his autobiography, Henderson addressed such claims by saying, "Yes, I'm a hot dog. Yes, I'm a showman. But remember, this is baseball. This is entertainment. I'm an entertainer. . . . Baseball was made to be fun." Indeed, Henderson could be controversial at times, but he left no doubt that he was one of the game's most talented, exciting, and productive players.

Noted baseball statistician Bill James put Henderson's career into perspective this way: "Somebody asked me: Did I think Rickey Henderson was a Hall of Famer? I told them, 'If you could split him in two, you'd have two Hall of Famers.' The greatest base stealer of all time, the greatest power/speed combination of all time (except maybe Barry Bonds), the greatest leadoff man of all time. . . . Without exaggerating one inch, you could find fifty Hall of Famers who, all taken together, don't own as many records, and as many *important* records, as Rickey Henderson."

Oakland's Own

Rickey Henderson was born in Chicago, Illinois, on Christmas Day, December 25, 1958. When it was time for his mother, Bobbie, to give birth, she telephoned his father, John Henley, to tell him to come home immediately because she needed to go to the hospital. Henley was out playing cards at the time and did not return home right away. When he finally arrived later that night, he put Bobbie in the car and started to drive to the hospital, but it was too late. Bobbie gave birth to Rickey in the rear seat of the car, a '57 Chevy. Throughout his career as a major-league player, Henderson always gave credit to his mother for taking care of him and raising him properly, and it all started from the moment she delivered him all by herself on the way to the hospital.

By the time Rickey was two years old, Henley had left the family for good. Bobbie moved her children to her mother's home in a small town called Pine Bluff in Arkansas. During his early childhood years, Rickey lived on his grandmother's farm. One activity that he did on the farm was run after the chickens, as he writes in his autobiography: "I'd chase them, then they'd chase me. Man, those chickens were fast. Put dozens of chickens together in one coop, and they run every which way. I had to be fast to keep up with them, but there wasn't a chicken on that entire farm that could outrun me. And I was teeney-weeney. I think that's when Momma realized I was going to be faster than most kids." Bobbie eventually decided to move her family to California. She had to find a house and a job first, so she went by herself to Oakland, California, and left the children in Arkansas with their grandmother. During this time in Oakland, Bobbie met and married a man named Paul Henderson. When Paul and Bobbie Henderson sent for the kids, the entire family moved to Oakland except for Rickey's youngest brother, who stayed in Arkansas with his grandmother.

Paul and Bobbie Henderson eventually separated, but that did not stop the Henderson children from growing up in a close family atmosphere. Henderson credits his mother for keeping the family together through good times and bad. "We've always been a close family, and Momma is the reason. She made sure we stayed close." Bobbie would ultimately have seven children, five boys and two girls.

THE KING OF BUSHROD PARK

Rickey played many sports while growing up, and he spent a lot of time at a place in his Oakland neighborhood called Bushrod Park. A home away from home, Bushrod Park was the perfect place to learn how to play all kinds of sports. Rickey eventually developed into one of the park's best players. When he was in the sixth grade, Rickey won his first trophy for being the park's Athlete of the Year. According to Henderson, "They'd give this huge trophy to the kid in the area who excelled the most in all sports, football, basketball, baseball, track. . . . I got the huge trophy. This thing was almost as tall as I was. I felt so proud. I was the king of Bushrod."

Rickey went to Oakland Technical High School, where he played many sports, including baseball and basketball. He ran a little track, too. In his junior year, he hit .716 on the baseball team, and the following season, Rickey batted .435 and stole 30 bases. His favorite sport, however, was football. With his speed and explosive running ability, Rickey was a great running back on his high school team. In fact, he was so good that people often compared him to O.J. Simpson, a running back who played high school football in San Francisco before becoming a Heisman Trophy winner at the University of Southern California and a Hall of Fame player in the National Football League.

Rickey was an excellent player, but his Oakland Tech team did not have much success until late in his senior year. In a game against the heavily favored Oakland High team, Rickey had one of his most memorable moments on the football field. Going into that game, Oakland Tech was on a terrible losing streak, and it seemed certain that the team would lose to its rival. Rickey, though, started the game off right by running back the opening kickoff 98 yards for a touchdown. His spectacular return helped motivate the team and propel it to victory in that game and in the rest of its games that season. Rickey would end up rushing for 1,100 yards in his senior season.

When he was in high school, Rickey dreamed of becoming an NFL running back for his hometown team, the Oakland Raiders. Known as "The Silver and Black," the Raiders were one of the league's best teams at the time. Rickey imagined going to a big-time college football program and becoming a superstar for the Raiders. As it turned out, Rickey was drafted by his hometown team in 1976, but that team was not the Oakland Raiders. Instead, Rickey was selected in the fourth round of the draft by his hometown baseball team, the Oakland Athletics. As exciting as it was to be drafted by the A's, Rickey faced one of the toughest decisions in his life. Should he stick with his dream of playing college and professional football, or should he sign a contract with the A's and start a professional baseball career?

Rickey ultimately left the choice up to the person who had been the biggest influence in his life. He asked his mother what he should do, and she told Rickey to play baseball. Bobbie worried that her son—at 5-foot-10 (178 centimeters)—was too small for football and that he could get hurt. Though he did not like the decision, Rickey respected his mother's choice and signed a minor-league contract with the Oakland A's. Rickey agreed to give baseball a fair shot, but he did not give up entirely on his football dream. He told himself that he would go back and pursue a football career if he was not playing major-league ball within four years.

STUDENT OF THE GAME

In the early 1970's, the Oakland A's were a baseball power-house, a mighty dynasty that won five consecutive division championships and three straight World Series (1972, 1973, and 1974). Charlie O. Finley, the owner of the A's back then, was an innovative owner, but he was also notoriously cheap when it came to paying salaries. In 1976, for example, a typical first-round draft pick could expect to receive a $100,000 signing bonus. Finley and the A's, on the other hand, paid their 1976 first-round pick only $17,500. Rickey was a fourth-round pick, so he knew he could expect even less. After graduating from Oakland Tech High School, the 17-year-old Henderson started his professional baseball career in the minor leagues on the Athletics' Class A team in Boise, Idaho.

★ ★ ★ ★ ★ ☆
THE SWINGIN' A'S DYNASTY
OF THE 1970s

In the early 1970s, the Oakland A's put together one of the most successful championship teams of all time. In 1972, the A's took on the heavily favored Cincinnati Reds in the World Series. The Series was very close, but the A's defeated the Reds in the seventh game to give Oakland its first-ever World Series championship. The title was also the franchise's first championship since 1930, when the team was based in Philadelphia. The A's went on to capture the next two World Series (1973 and 1974) to earn a rare spot in baseball history by winning back-to-back-to-back World Series.

The A's dynasty of the 1970s was unique. The team featured many outstanding players as well as many colorful personalities, like slugger Reggie Jackson, pitcher Jim "Catfish" Hunter, and reliever Rollie Fingers. In 1972, owner Charlie O. Finley told his players that he would pay an extra $500 to anyone on the club who grew a mustache as part of a Mustache Day promotion. From that point on, the A's became known for their facial hair, even though they played at a time when baseball teams typically required players to be clean-shaven. The A's also took to wearing colorful uniforms when the other major-league teams donned plain, simple uniforms. They wore solid green or gold jerseys with contrasting white pants.

Unfortunately, the great A's dynasty did not stay together long after their third World Series championship. Unwilling to pay the high salaries required to keep his stars, Finley began to sell off his players or let them go as free agents. Thus, the owner responsible for building the Swingin' A's into a baseball powerhouse was also the man most responsible for dismantling the dynasty.

The Oakland A's celebrated their win after defeating the Cincinnati Reds in the 1972 World Series, the first of three straight titles for the Swingin' A's dynasty of the 1970s. Rickey Henderson was a young teenager growing up in Oakland at the time.

Rickey's first contract paid him $500 a month in addition to a one-time signing bonus of $10,000.

Rickey joined the Boise team in midseason and played in 46 games. He proved right away that he was a good hitter and a superior base stealer. Rickey was a naturally talented athlete, but he also understood the importance of working hard to become an even better ballplayer. In his first years in the minor leagues, for example, he needed to improve his defensive skills in the outfield. At Boise, Rickey led the league

☆ ☆ ☆ ☆ ☆ ☆

AN EYE FOR GREATNESS

In baseball terms, having a good eye means having the ability to tell the difference between balls and strikes while standing in the batter's box. Rickey Henderson had a great eye, and one of his strengths as a ballplayer was his ability to draw a base on balls, or a walk. According to Tom Trebelhorn, one of Henderson's minor-league managers, Henderson had this skill from the time he arrived in the minors. "He had the best idea of a strike zone at 17 years of age of anybody I've had anywhere. . . . Henderson walked, he did not swing at bad pitches. That same ability carried him to the all-time record in bases on balls, runs scored, stolen bases. He was a terrific player at 17 and 18. . . . He was a man, and from there he was in the big leagues in a couple of years at 20."

Henderson led the American League in walks on four occasions (1982, 1983, 1989, and 1998). He drew more than 100 walks a year seven times in his career, and finished in the top 10 in walks in 16 seasons between 1980 and 1998. On April 25, 2001, while playing for the San Diego Padres, Henderson notched the 2,063rd walk of his career, moving him ahead of Babe Ruth as baseball's all-time walks leader. Henderson's record for most walks was broken by San Francisco Giants slugger Barry Bonds in 2004. An interesting note is that Bonds accumulated many walks intentionally because pitchers did not want him to hit home runs. Henderson, on the other hand, rarely received an intentional pass because pitchers desperately wanted to keep him off base, where he could take over a game with his running ability. Henderson is currently in second place on the all-time list with 2,190 walks for his career. Bonds had 2,558 walks through the 2007 season.

with 12 outfield errors, even though he was only on the team for part of the season. Likewise, in Modesto the following year, he led the league in outfield errors. Most of Rickey's errors were throwing errors, so he worked especially hard to improve this part of his game. Specifically, he did not have a particularly strong throwing arm, so he learned how to use his speed to take the quickest angle of approach to the ball. Over time his hard work paid off. The following year, 1978, while playing Class AA ball in Jersey City, New Jersey, Rickey not only cut down on his outfield errors, but he also led the league in outfield assists and double plays.

Rickey was a hard worker in the minor leagues. He also improved his game by learning from his minor-league coaches and teammates. One of his coaches, Lee Walls, helped Rickey improve his defense, and he also taught Rickey the value of studying some of the game's greatest players, including legendary base stealers like Ty Cobb, Maury Wills, and Lou Brock. Rickey learned a great deal by studying what made these players successful.

He also learned from some of his minor-league teammates, including a catcher named Mike Rodriguez. Rodriguez was not a fast player, but he always ran as hard as he could and he always looked for opportunities to take an extra base by stretching singles into doubles and doubles into triples. In addition, few players at the time slid headfirst, but Rodriguez believed it made the difference between being safe or out on close plays. Rickey also came to appreciate the value of sliding in this manner. He liked the headfirst slide because it saved his legs from the constant pounding they endured from sliding feetfirst all the time. He also liked to slide this way because it added a new element of excitement and showmanship to his game. Over time, Rickey perfected the headfirst slide to the point that it became one of his signature moves.

Rickey Henderson dove toward third base as Jack Howell of the California Angels caught the ball during a game in April 1991. During his minor-league years, Henderson perfected the headfirst slide and made it one of his signature moves.

One of Rickey's first minor-league managers was Tom Trebelhorn, who led Boise and Modesto in 1976 and 1977. Later, Trebelhorn went on to manage the Milwaukee Brewers and the Chicago Cubs. In the minor leagues, Trebelhorn helped Rickey develop his base-stealing skills. According to Rickey, "Treb taught me much about stealing. He used to drag me out to the park at one o'clock before night games just to teach me how to steal bases. He'd stand on the mound and imitate the pitcher, giving me every move in the book. He knew his stuff and was a workhorse when it came time to teaching kids how to play baseball. He took not only his work time but his free time to teach us. He was a real manager, a true teacher."

Trebelhorn recognized Rickey's talent and quickly learned how to best use his speedy young player. On Trebelhorn's team in Modesto, for instance, Rickey led the league with 95 steals for the year, which was the record in the California League at the time. He once stole seven bases in one game. Trebelhorn knew he had a player with exceptional skills: "I let him run; that was it. He could run; he was going to be a good base stealer, a good player—I let him play. The things we worked on were fairly routine, but he was a great student. He came early, he wanted to do well, to get to the big leagues and be a great player."

Rickey started the 1979 season with the Athletics' Class AAA club in Ogden, Utah. Then, in June, he received the call he had been waiting for. The A's needed him to fill in for an injured player. It had been a little more than three years since Rickey graduated from Oakland Tech High School and signed his first minor-league contract. Now he was returning to his hometown as a starting outfielder for the Oakland Athletics.

Hometown Hero

When the A's drafted Rickey Henderson out of high school in 1976, they were still one of the best teams in baseball, but that changed in a hurry. By the time Henderson was called up to the ball club in 1979, the A's had become one of the league's worst teams. They were 22–50 and in last place in the American League West when Henderson joined the team. In his first big-league game, on June 24, 1979, Henderson clubbed two hits and stole the first base of his major-league career. He played well, but the team lost—a pattern that would be a familiar one throughout the season. Henderson had a good year, but the team was terrible, losing 108 games. Henderson played in 89 games for the 1979 A's (a little more than half the season). He finished with a respectable .274 batting average and had nearly 100 hits. He also proved right away that

Rickey Henderson slid past the tag by catcher Thurman Munson to score against the Yankees in a game on July 20, 1979, during Henderson's rookie year. In his next season, Henderson would swipe 100 bases—setting a new American League record.

he was a force on the base paths by leading the team with 33 steals. Henderson played well enough to show everyone that he belonged in the big leagues, but his rookie season was nothing compared with what he would do the following year.

In 1980, Henderson really took off, and the A's turned their game around. Led by fiery new manager Billy Martin, Oakland played an aggressive and exciting style of baseball called "BillyBall." The A's did not have the biggest stars, but Martin knew how to get the best out of his young talent. In particular, he knew how to get the best out of his speedy young outfielder. Henderson ran wild in 1980 and finished the season with 100 steals, which broke Ty Cobb's American League record for most steals in a year. Henderson was the first American League player and only the third player in major-league history to steal at least 100 bases in a season. In one interview, Martin pointed out that, while Henderson was setting an individual record, he was also helping the team. "Of his 100 stolen bases," Martin said, "I'd bet 95 of them meant something."

Also in 1980, Henderson hit for an excellent .303 average, walked 117 times, and scored 111 runs. His great play and the

★ ★ ★ ★ ★ ☆

THE PROUDEST YANKEE

Billy Martin played for and managed a number of different teams during his major-league career, but he was first and foremost a New York Yankee. Martin's career with the Yankees began in 1950, when he signed on to play second base for New York after playing for two years with the Oakland Oaks of the Pacific Coast League. Known for his aggressive playing style and for coming through in clutch situations, Martin also had a reputation for causing controversy on and off the field. For instance, a party on his twenty-ninth birthday at New York's famous Copacabana night club ended in a brawl. Highlights from his playing days include being named to the All-Star team in 1956 and winning the Most Valuable Player award of the 1953 World Series. He retired as a player in 1961.

As a manager, Martin led four different American League teams to division championships—the Minnesota Twins, the Detroit Tigers, the New York Yankees, and the Oakland A's. With team's aggressive strategy paid off in victories. After finishing in last place the previous year, Oakland moved all the way up to second place in the American League West. In his first full season in the majors, Henderson also earned his first trip to the All-Star Game.

The Athletics' prospects looked even better going into the 1981 season. After trying to sell the team for quite some time, owner Charlie O. Finley finally found a buyer—the Haas family. The sale was good news for many reasons. There had been speculation that Finley would sell the team to an out-of-town buyer who would move the A's away from Oakland. The Haas family, however, was committed to keeping the team in

☆ ☆ ☆ ☆ ☆ ☆

the Yankees, he won the 1977 World Series. He was a great manager, though he was often involved in turmoil. He was quick to lose his temper and became famous for his animated arguments with umpires. He also had a long-running love-hate relationship with New York Yankees owner George Steinbrenner. Steinbrenner hired Martin five different times to manage the Yankees. He also fired him five times.

Regardless of their problems, on August 10, 1986, Steinbrenner and the Yankees honored Martin for his accomplishments as a player and manager by retiring his uniform (No. 1) and dedicating a special plaque in his honor at Yankee Stadium. On the day he received this honor, Martin said, "I may not have been the greatest Yankee to ever put on a uniform, but I am the proudest."

Martin died in an automobile accident on December 25, 1989, the same day as Rickey Henderson's thirty-first birthday.

the East Bay. In addition, they were also prepared to spend more money to build a winning franchise. During the last years of Finley's ownership, the A's had lost many great players because Finley did not want to spend the money to keep them. The new owners did not share this philosophy. After the success of the previous season and with new ownership in place, Oakland entered the 1981 season with high hopes.

The A's blew out of the starting gate in 1981, winning their first 11 games with a combination of great starting pitching and an aggressive wide-open offense led by Henderson. Behind the scenes, however, Major League Baseball was facing enormous labor problems, mainly over the issue of free agency, and in the middle of the season the players went on a strike that canceled all games for 50 days. When the strike was finally settled, Major League Baseball needed to make up for lost time, so baseball officials shortened the season and split it into two parts. Each division would have two winners—the winner of the first half of the season and the winner of the second half. In the American League West, the A's won the first half of the season, while the Kansas City Royals won the second half. This set up a divisional play-off series between the two teams. The A's won the West by sweeping the Royals in three games to earn the right to meet the New York Yankees in the American League Championship Series. Unfortunately for the A's, their season came to an abrupt end when they lost the championship series in three games.

Henderson was terrific throughout the strike-interrupted season, and he continued to play great in the postseason. Though the A's were disappointed by the play-off loss to New York, they had to feel good that they had come so far in such a short amount of time. Just two years after being one of the league's worst teams, Oakland had come very close to making it to the World Series. Henderson played a huge part in the team's turnaround. In fact, he nearly won the American

League Most Valuable Player award, coming in second place behind Rollie Fingers, the former A's relief pitcher who was now playing for the Milwaukee Brewers. Henderson finished the season with a .319 batting average, scoring 89 runs and stealing 56 bases. He also won a Gold Glove for his outstanding play in left field. After a little more than two seasons with the Athletics, Henderson had established himself as one of the league's best players.

THE BIRTH OF BILLYBALL

Sportswriter Ralph Wiley came up with the term "BillyBall" to describe the way Billy Martin managed the A's. Wiley would later go on to write many books and have a successful career as a journalist for magazines like *Sports Illustrated* as well as for the *Page 2* section of ESPN.com. While covering the A's for the *Oakland Tribune*, Wiley had the opportunity to witness and write about the dynamic new brand of baseball being played by the East Bay team. As Billy Martin explained in his book *BillyBall*:

> A writer in Oakland came up with the term (BillyBall). It wasn't that I was doing anything different in Oakland from what I did everywhere else I managed. Everywhere I have played, for that matter. But this writer, Ralph Wiley, watched us win games with the double steal, with aggressive base running, with the suicide squeeze. He watched us gamble and take chances. He watched us try things that upset the opposition, forced them into making errors. He watched all this stuff, and it was successful, and one day he referred to this daring style of play as "BillyBall." Then it just caught on. Other writers started using it. They started using it on radio and TV. And the next thing you know, the Oakland club jumped on the slogan and began to use it in its promotional and advertising campaigns.

Oakland A's manager Billy Martin argued with the umpire during a game in 1982. Martin's exciting style of baseball, with a focus on aggressive base running, was dubbed "BillyBall" during his tenure in Oakland. And Rickey Henderson was the ideal player for BillyBall.

Martin might have managed all his teams the same way, but there was one huge difference between his other teams and his Oakland team. The difference was Rickey Henderson. If any player was built to thrive in a system that focused on an aggressive and disruptive running game, it was Henderson. Martin clearly knew he had a special player, and he looked for ways to take advantage of Henderson's extraordinary skills. As Martin put it, "He became my offensive leader, and I managed around him. If Rickey got on base, we produced runs. It was as simple as that. I let Rickey run. Every chance he got, he was stealing. I had one of the game's greatest base stealers of all time, so I took advantage of his skill." BillyBall was fun and exciting for the players and the fans, and, most important, it resulted in wins.

As Henderson put it in his book, *Off Base: Confessions of a Thief*:

> We didn't beat teams because we had a powerful offense. We beat them with trickery. If we couldn't knock home a run, we'd steal it. We'd run at every opportunity. Our aggressive style became known as BillyBall. When people thought of BillyBall, they thought of his wild, open-air style of managing. Billy was the publisher of BillyBall, and I was the author. It was a marriage made in heaven. Oh, that was fun. That was an exciting club.

A RECORD YEAR FOR "THE MAN OF STEAL"

Henderson met Lou Brock for the first time during the 1981 season. At the time, Brock held the two most important stolen-base records in baseball. He was the major leagues' all-time steals leader (with 938 career stolen bases), and he also held the record for most steals in a season (he stole 118 bases in 1974). From the time of their first meeting, Brock recognized Henderson's talents and believed that Henderson would break his records. Henderson and Brock met again after the 1981 season. This time, Henderson spent a few days with the base-stealing champion and learned as much as he could. Henderson was already a successful ballplayer, but he knew he could get even better by learning from Brock.

After nearly making it to the World Series in 1981, the A's had very high expectations heading into the following season. In spring training, Martin told Henderson that the team was going to run even more and that Henderson should take aim at Brock's single-season stolen-bases record. Two years earlier, Henderson had stolen 100 bases and broken Ty Cobb's American League record, so he knew the major-league record was not impossible. He also knew that he would have to deliver an incredible performance to have any chance. Martin helped Henderson go after the record by changing his managerial philosophy somewhat for the 1982 season. In their previous seasons together, Martin did not allow Henderson to run on his own in every situation. In 1982, however, Martin gave Henderson more freedom to run just about whenever he wanted. The strategy paid off. By the All-Star break, Henderson already had 84 steals. Barring injury, he was well on his way to breaking Brock's single-season record.

As Henderson chased the record, fans came to the ballpark in great numbers to witness his historic run. Henderson and

☆ ☆ ☆ ☆ ☆ ☆

"THE RUNNING REDBIRD"

Lou Brock was Major League Baseball's stolen-base king before Rickey Henderson came along. After starting his career with the Chicago Cubs in 1961, Brock and two other players were traded in 1964 to the St. Louis Cardinals for three players, including a pitcher named Ernie Broglio. It was one of the best trades in Cardinal history and one of the worst for the Cubs. In 19 years in the major leagues, Brock was the National League stolen-base leader eight times, was voted onto the All-Star team six times, and led the Cardinals to three World Series appearances (they won twice). Brock was a great clutch hitter, especially in the World Series. In 1974, Brock broke the record for most stolen bases in a year with 118. That same year, he finished second in voting for the league's Most Valuable Player award behind Los Angeles Dodgers first baseman Steve Garvey. Brock retired in 1979.

Brock overcame tremendous odds to make it to the big leagues. According to Brock's Web site, he "grew up in Collinston, Louisiana, on a poverty-stricken cotton plantation

Martin tried to set it up so that the record-breaking steal would happen in front of the hometown fans at the Oakland Coliseum. Unfortunately, they could not pull it off. Henderson ended a long homestand in August just one stolen base short of the record. Then, on August 27, 1982, in a road game against the Milwaukee Brewers, Henderson took off in an attempt to steal his 119th base of the season. Guessing that Henderson would be off and running, the Brewers had called a pitchout, which is a pitch deliberately thrown out of the reach of the batter so that the catcher can throw out a base runner. The pitchout did not matter. Henderson was safe; the record was his.

☆ ☆ ☆ ☆ ☆ ☆

where he picked and chopped cotton to help his family survive. . . . After the first semester at Southern University, he lost his acquired academic scholarship when he received a C+ rather than the required B average. During the semester break, he lived on campus with friends and volunteered to retrieve balls for the college baseball team. One day . . . the coaches rewarded him for his effort with five batting-practice swings. He promptly hit three of the five balls over the fence and was given a full baseball scholarship on the spot."

Known as "The Running Redbird," Brock was inducted into the Baseball Hall of Fame in 1985. His Hall of Fame plaque reads: "Baseball's all-time leader in stolen bases with 938. Set major league record by stealing over 50 bases 12 times and N.L. record with 118 steals in 1974. Led N.L. in stolen bases 8 times. Collected 3,023 hits during 19 year career and holds World Series record with .391 batting average in 21 post-season games."

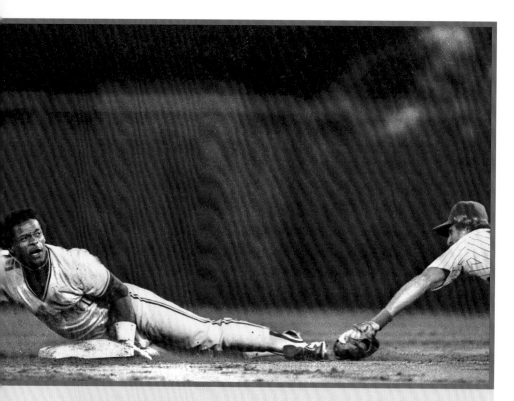

Rickey Henderson held on to second base as he captured his 119th stolen base of the 1982 season during a game on August 27 in Milwaukee. With the stolen base, Henderson broke Lou Brock's season record. Henderson ended 1982 with 130 steals.

During a short ceremony, Henderson expressed his appreciation for teammate Dwayne Murphy, who hit second in the lineup. Murphy's was the key position in the batting order because he had to take a lot of pitches and sacrifice a lot of at-bats to give Henderson the best chance to steal. Henderson had brought some of his family, including his mother, Bobbie, to watch his record-breaking performance. Lou Brock was also in attendance to congratulate the man who broke his record. Henderson ended up stealing four bases that day, but the A's lost the game, 5-4, to the Brewers.

He finished the season with 130 stolen bases, nearly 80 steals ahead of his closest competitor in the American League.

Henderson's run for the record in 1982 was remarkable. Unfortunately, the team did not have the same success. One year after making it to the American League Championship Series, Oakland finished in fifth place in the American League West with a 68–94 record. After the season, the A's fired Martin. The BillyBall era was officially over in Oakland. For the next two seasons, Henderson would continue to play at a high level, making the All-Star team both years. The A's, however, did not get any better. Oakland finished in fourth place in 1983 and 1984.

After the 1984 season, the A's had to rebuild. They also had to face the fact that Henderson was going to be a free agent. Instead of trying to re-sign Henderson, the A's traded their superstar to the New York Yankees. It was a bittersweet trade for Henderson. He was leaving his hometown club, but he was excited at the prospect of showcasing his skills in New York. Billy Martin was not the manager of the Yankees at the time, but he had close connections with owner George Steinbrenner and worked behind the scenes to urge Steinbrenner to make a deal for Henderson. Martin later explained it this way:

> "Look, George," I said. "You have to make this deal. I know you're giving up Jay Howell and three young pitchers, but young pitchers are a dime a dozen. You can always replace them. They come along all the time. A Rickey Henderson comes along once in a lifetime. Believe me, if you get Rickey Henderson, he's going to make the difference in the whole ball club. He'll make Don Mattingly better. He'll make Dave Winfield better. He'll help everybody. Please, George. If I'm wrong, then fire me. I feel that strongly about this trade. I know this kid that well." . . . And so the Rickey Henderson deal was made, and I'm here to tell you

that Rickey is a once-in-a-lifetime player. You see very few Rickey Hendersons. You might not see another one for fifty years.

After establishing himself as a big-league star in Oakland, Henderson was on his way to baseball's biggest stage—New York.

In the
Big Apple

The first World Series in major-league history took place in 1903. Since then, the Fall Classic, as the World Series is sometimes called, has been played nearly every year to determine baseball's ultimate champion. In 1923, the New York Yankees won their first World Series. Since then, the Yankees have accumulated 26 championships, more titles than any other team by far. (The St. Louis Cardinals are in second place with 10 World Series trophies.) Over the years, the Yankees have not only become baseball's most successful franchise, but they are quite possibly the premier sports franchise in the United States. Some of the greatest ballplayers in history have played for the New York Yankees, including Babe Ruth, Lou Gehrig, Joe DiMaggio, Mickey Mantle, Whitey Ford, and

Yogi Berra. These players, and many others, helped build the Yankees into a baseball dynasty.

When George Steinbrenner became the owner of the Yankees in the 1970s, he sought to build great Yankee teams, in part, by spending huge sums of money to lure free-agent superstars. On December 8, 1984, Steinbrenner acquired Rickey Henderson. The A's traded Henderson and pitcher Bert Bradley to the Yankees for outfielder Stan Javier and four pitchers, Jay Howell, José Rijo, Tim Birtsas, and Eric Plunk. In his five years with Oakland, Henderson had done many great things on the baseball field, but he had not accomplished his primary goal of winning the World Series. By moving to the Yankees, Henderson was joining an incredible team with a legitimate shot at World Series glory. He was rewarded with a five-year contract worth more than $8.5 million, making him the third-highest-paid player in baseball at the time. He certainly had come a long way from the day he signed his first minor-league deal for $500 a month and a $10,000 signing bonus. Expectations for the Yankees ran very high when Henderson joined the club. New York featured a lineup stacked with some of the game's most talented players, including Don Mattingly, Don Baylor, Willie Randolph, Ken Griffey, and Dave Winfield. This team, its fans, and the owner all expected not only to reach the play-offs but also to win the World Series.

Henderson's start with the Yankees did not go as smoothly as he would have liked. He hurt his ankle in spring training and missed the first 10 games of the regular season. Then, as Henderson and his teammates were getting to know one another, they had to deal with a totally unexpected managerial change. In a move that surprised just about everyone, Steinbrenner fired manager Yogi Berra after only the sixteenth game of the season. Even more surprisingly, Steinbrenner replaced him with Billy Martin, who had previously managed the Yankees from 1975 to 1978 and in 1979.

Rickey Henderson took a lead off first base as Rod Carew of the Angels tried to keep him close to the bag during a game in 1985, which was Henderson's first season with the New York Yankees. Henderson finished third in the voting for the American League MVP that year.

As it turned out, Henderson had even more problems to deal with during his first year with the Yankees. In fact, his difficulties with the press began from the day he arrived at Yankee Stadium. As Henderson states in his autobiography, "When I opened the clubhouse door, I was swarmed by a mob of reporters. There were dozens upon dozens of people with notepads and microphones and bright camera lights. I wasn't expecting such a wild scene. I was a 26-year-old ballplayer, and I hadn't ever seen anything like that. . . . I made my way through the crowd of reporters and blared out, 'I don't need no press now, man.'" Henderson just wanted to get on the field and start working with his new team, but many in the press took his words the wrong way and were put off by his attitude. Even though Henderson was an established big-league player who was used to dealing with the media, he learned quickly that he had to deal with the press much differently in New York than he did in Oakland.

☆ ☆ ☆ ☆ ☆ ☆

"DONNIE BASEBALL"

Don Mattingly was one of Rickey Henderson's favorite team-mates on the New York Yankees. During the mid- to late 1980s, Mattingly was a six-time All-Star and arguably the best player in all of baseball. In 1984, he won the American League batting title with a .343 average. The race for the batting crown went down to the last game of the season, when Mattingly went four-for-five to finish just ahead of teammate Dave Winfield. That same year, Mattingly also led the league with 207 hits; he hit 23 home runs and drove in 110 RBIs. In 1985, he had an even better year, win-ning the American League MVP award by hitting .324 with 35 homers and 145 RBIs. He almost was named MVP again in 1986, finishing second in the voting after batting .352 with 31 home runs and 113 RBIs. He lost that year to pitcher Roger Clemens of the Boston Red Sox. Mattingly, who played for 14 seasons, had a lifetime batting average of .307. He finished his career with 2,153 hits, 222 home runs, and 1,099 RBIs.

Indeed, Mattingly was one of the greatest Yankees ever, but he also had the misfortune of playing for the franchise

SO CLOSE, SO FAR

As soon as his ankle healed, Henderson began to show everyone in New York why he was such a valuable player. After starting off slowly at the plate, he caught fire and had one of the best all-around seasons of his career. In 1985, Henderson scored a league-leading 146 runs. He also stole 80 bases to lead the American League and break a Yankee team record for steals that had stood for 71 years. He hit for an excellent .314 average and had 24 home runs, the first time in his career that

during a time when it did not play in any World Series. He joined the Yankees in 1982, just after they won the 1981 World Series, and he retired the year before they played again in another World Series. In fact, Mattingly only reached the postseason once.

In 1995, Mattingly and the Yankees faced the Seattle Mariners in the American League Division Series. Mattingly hit .417 and knocked in six RBIs during the series, but the Yankees lost in five games. Mattingly did not play again after that. On August 31, 1997, the Yankees retired Don Mattingly's number and dedicated a plaque to him in Monument Park at Yankee Stadium.

After the 2003 season, the Yankees named Mattingly as their hitting coach. In October 2006, he was promoted to being manager Joe Torre's bench coach. After the 2007 season, Torre left the Yankees and became manager of the Los Angeles Dodgers. When the Yankees did not hire Mattingly as their new manager, he followed Torre to Los Angeles to be the Dodgers' hitting coach.

he hit more than 20 homers. In fact, Henderson became the first player in American League history to hit more than 20 home runs and steal more than 50 bases in the same year. For the second time in his career, he came very close to winning the American League MVP award. Henderson finished third in voting for the MVP award, which was won by his teammate Don Mattingly. Though the Yankees were an explosive club on offense, they had a weakness—their pitching. Even with all the offensive firepower, New York could not win its division. The team battled hard all season and had a chance to make the play-offs right up to the very last series of the year. Unfortunately for the Yankees, they finished in second place in the American League East behind the Toronto Blue Jays and missed the play-offs.

Steinbrenner has a reputation for being an owner who spends a lot of money to build his team. He is also known for being an impatient owner who is never satisfied with second place. After the Yankees failed to make the play-offs in 1985, Steinbrenner made another one of his patented managerial changes, this time replacing Billy Martin with Lou Piniella. Henderson had already had three managers in New York, and it was only the start of his second season with the team. Despite the changes, the Yankees continued to have sky-high expectations going into the 1986 season. Even with a new manager, however, the team played out a familiar story. Many Yankee players performed well during the season. For instance, Henderson, Mattingly, and Dave Winfield all made the All-Star team for the second year in a row. Again, though, the team's pitching was not of the same quality as the offense, and for the second straight year the Yankees finished in second place in the American League East, this time behind the Boston Red Sox.

In 1986, Henderson continued to play at a high level and rack up excellent statistics. For the seventh straight year, he led the American League in steals. He also had career highs

One of Rickey Henderson's favorite teammates on the Yankees was Don Mattingly, known as "Donnie Baseball." Mattingly had a string of great seasons during the mid- to late 1980s, but he also had the misfortune of never reaching the World Series.

up to that point in home runs (28), doubles (31), and RBIs (74). In his first two years on the Yankees, Henderson proved that he could not only survive the pressure of playing in New York, but that he could also thrive on baseball's biggest stage.

★ ★ ★ ★ ★ ★

THE ALL-STAR GAME GOES EXTRA INNINGS

Rickey Henderson made the All-Star team 10 times in his first 13 seasons. On July 14, 1987, Henderson played in one of the most memorable All-Star Games in major-league history. The game was played at the Oakland Coliseum, the site of so many of Henderson's past highlights. Even though he was on the Yankees at the time, Henderson must have felt a great deal of pride playing in the All-Star Game in front of his hometown fans. The game was also special for Henderson because he was joined on the All-Star team by four Yankee teammates: Dave Winfield, Don Mattingly, Willie Randolph, and Dave Righetti. Although many great hitters were on the American and National League rosters, this game turned out to be one of the best pitching duels in All-Star Game history.

Pitchers on both teams kept the game scoreless through 12 innings. By that time, Henderson had long been replaced, so he had to watch the dramatic conclusion from the dugout. The American League almost won the game in exciting fashion in the ninth inning when Winfield tried to score on an infield grounder. Unfortunately, Winfield was gunned down at the plate. This set the stage for further drama in the thirteenth inning. With two runners on base, Tim Raines of the Montreal Expos hit a triple that knocked in the game's only two runs. The National League won, and Raines was named the game's MVP for his clutch performance.

Though the Yankees failed again to reach the play-offs, the ball club believed that it had the talent to win it all and looked forward to proving it the next season. Little did Henderson and his teammates know that the past two seasons would be as good as it would get for this group of Yankees. The team was headed for hard times, and, for the first time in his career, so was Rickey Henderson.

INJURY AND CONFLICT

Henderson had been spectacular in his first two years as a Yankee, and he was determined to perform at an even higher level in 1987. Sure enough, he came out of spring training on fire and ripped up the league during the first two months of the season. By May 30, he was batting .327. He was on his way to having his best season ever, but then a leg injury brought his year to a sudden stop. Until this point in his career, Henderson had not missed a significant number of games because of injury or any other reason. That all changed. After missing five games, Henderson tried to come back on June 4 and help the team even though his leg was not entirely healed. In his first game back, Henderson took off to steal second base and felt a terrible pain in his leg. It hurt so bad that Henderson had to leave the game. At first, the injury was diagnosed as a strained hamstring, and Henderson was put on the disabled list. The team was optimistic that he would be back after two weeks of rest.

The injury, though, lingered for much longer than two weeks. Henderson returned to play at the end of June, but his leg still did not feel right, and he could not do what he was used to doing on the field. Henderson was playing, but the injury really slowed him down. To make matters worse, articles started to appear in the New York newspapers speculating about the seriousness of the injury. Some stories even claimed that Henderson was not seriously injured and was faking it so he could take time off. Instead of focusing on getting healthy

Rickey Henderson, shown here at the plate in 1988, made an impressive comeback that year—hitting .305 and stealing 93 bases. Henderson's 1987 season had been marred by a leg injury as well as by speculation about the seriousness of that injury.

and trying to help the team, Henderson was caught in the middle of a huge media controversy. Throughout his career, Henderson had always played hard and done all he could to help his team win. Now, however, everything was going against him. Henderson played for more than a month on the injured leg. Unfortunately, the pain did not go away and neither did the flak. The Yankees eventually sent Henderson to another doctor to get a second opinion. The new doctor discovered that the injury was much more serious than a strain and that Henderson had a partially torn hamstring. Furthermore, the leg was not going to heal without extended rest, so Henderson once again went on the disabled list. He rested the leg and came back with about a month left in the season. The Yankees still had a chance to make the play-offs when Henderson returned, but they fell short and finished the season in fourth place in the American League East. Besides the fallout over Henderson's injury, the Yankees had to deal with another controversy throughout the year. Lou Piniella and owner George Steinbrenner had been engaged in an ongoing feud, which led to Piniella's firing at the end of the season. All in all, there were too many distractions for the club to overcome. In 1987, Henderson only played in 95 games, and for the first time in his career he did not lead the league in steals.

After the disastrous 1987 campaign, Henderson was eager to come into spring training healthy. He wanted to put the injury behind him and once again show the baseball world that he was one of the game's most productive players. Sure enough, Henderson returned to form. He hit .305 in 1988 and again led the league in steals (with 93 stolen bases). Even though Henderson stayed healthy and played well, the Yankees did not have a good year. Moreover, the team was once again dogged by managerial changes. After firing Piniella, Steinbrenner brought back Billy Martin to manage the ball club. Then, in the middle of the season, Steinbrenner did an about-face by firing Martin and rehiring Piniella as manager. Throughout all of the managerial turmoil, Henderson continued to play well. The Yankees, though, went on a major skid after the All-Star break to finish in fifth place. This, of course, did not sit well with Steinbrenner, who again fired Piniella, replacing him this time with Dallas Green.

Glory Days

Rickey Henderson got off to a slow start in 1989, and so did the Yankees. After two particularly bad seasons and a long playoff drought, New York needed to rebuild. Many of Henderson's past teammates were either traded or on the injured list. As for Henderson, his contract with the Yankees was set to expire at the end of the year, so he played knowing that this season might be his last in the Big Apple. As the season progressed and as the Yankees dropped further in the standings, trade rumors began to circulate. Henderson's contract included a no-trade option, which meant he could reject any trade he did not like. The situation had to be perfect for him to accept a trade; otherwise, he could stay with the Yankees for the rest of the year and then become a free agent and go to any team. There was talk that Henderson might end up with the San Francisco Giants, but nothing came of it.

The Yankees eventually worked out the perfect deal for Henderson by sending him back to Oakland on June 21. In exchange for Henderson, the Yankees received outfielder Luis Polonia and two pitchers, Greg Cadaret and Eric Plunk. In a little more than four seasons with New York, Henderson had had to deal with his share of controversy, but overall he had been very productive, except during his injury-plagued 1987 season. In the end, however, he had not won a World Series. It was difficult to leave the Yankees without accomplishing this goal, but Henderson had the satisfaction of knowing that he was returning home and joining a team that many had picked to win it all.

When Henderson returned to the A's, the team was in first place in the American League West. The club was already a very good one, and adding the game's best leadoff hitter made Oakland even stronger. Besides being a talented squad, the A's were extremely focused on winning the World Series because they just missed winning it the previous year against the Los Angeles Dodgers. The Dodgers had set the tone for their victory in the first game of that Series when Kirk Gibson, who was not even supposed to play because of injury, limped up to bat as a pinch hitter and struck one of the most memorable walk-off homers in baseball history. That one improbable swing seemed to give the Dodgers all the momentum they needed to steamroll over the heavily favored A's, four games to one. Losing to the Dodgers in 1988 was very disappointing for Oakland. When Henderson rejoined the Athletics, he was coming to a very talented team—a team that was just as determined as he was to win baseball's top prize.

When players are traded in the middle of a season, it often takes time for them to fit in with the new team. This was not the case when Henderson returned to Oakland in 1989. After struggling early in the season with the Yankees, Henderson immediately picked up his game in Oakland. In 65 games with the Yankees, Henderson had hit .247. With the A's, however, he increased his average to nearly .300 in 85 games and finished the regular season with a combined batting average of .274. He was also first in the American League in walks, steals, and runs scored. Before adding Henderson to their lineup, the A's already had a powerful offense that featured José Canseco, Mark McGwire, Dave "The Cobra" Parker, Dave "Hendu" Henderson, Terry Steinbach, and Carney Lansford. The potent A's arsenal, however, did not include much of a running game. That changed when Henderson

☆ ☆ ☆ ☆ ☆ ☆
THE BASH BROTHERS

The era of the "Bash Brothers" in Oakland started in 1987, when José Canseco and Mark McGwire combined to hit 80 home runs for the A's. The Oakland team of that era featured many excellent players, but Canseco and McGwire provided the powerful one-two punch at the heart of the batting order. Led by their two young sluggers, the A's became known as the "Bash Brothers" for hitting titanic home runs as well as for bashing their forearms together when crossing home plate.

McGwire and Canseco went on to put up some phenomenal numbers in their big-league careers. In 1988, for instance, Canseco won the American League MVP award by becoming the first player ever to hit at least 40 homers and steal 40 bases in the same year. After leaving the A's, he bounced around a number of teams, finishing his career with 462 home runs. As for McGwire, the A's traded him in 1997 to the St. Louis Cardinals. As a Cardinal, he broke Roger Maris's longstanding record (61) joined the team. Now opposing pitchers not only had to contend with some of the game's most fearsome sluggers, but they also had to keep baseball's best base stealer off the bases. With Henderson kick-starting the offense, Oakland took control of the American League West and won the division by seven games over the Kansas City Royals.

A CHAMPIONSHIP SERIES FOR THE AGES

When the play-offs started, the A's were determined not to suffer another disappointing postseason loss. Before the team could get back to the World Series, Oakland first had to go through the Toronto Blue Jays in the American League

☆ ☆ ☆ ☆ ☆

for most home runs in a season, hitting 70 in 1998. McGwire retired after the 2001 season with 583 career home runs, which ranks eighth on the all-time list behind Barry Bonds, Hank Aaron, Babe Ruth, Willie Mays, Sammy Sosa, Ken Griffey, Jr., and Frank Robinson.

Unfortunately for these two "Bash Brothers," they will not only go down in history for their many home runs but also for their connection to baseball's steroid scandal. Canseco later admitted taking steroids and accused many others—including McGwire—of taking performance-enhancing drugs. Since his retirement, McGwire has mostly led a quiet life out of the spotlight. In 2005, Canseco, McGwire, and several other baseball players appeared before a congressional committee to answer questions about the problem of steroids in baseball. McGwire did not answer questions about steroid use during his career, saying he was "not here to talk about the past."

Rickey Henderson's Oakland teammates congratulated him during Game 4 of the 1989 American League Championship Series against Toronto. In that game, Henderson hit two home runs. He was named the MVP of the series.

Championship Series. The first two games were played at the Oakland Coliseum. In Game 1, Henderson set the tone for the entire series without even getting a hit. He walked twice and stole two bases, but his biggest play came in the sixth inning. With Oakland losing 3-2 and two men on base, Henderson came up and was hit by a pitch to load the bases. As Henderson took his lead from first base, he was determined to get a good jump. The next batter hit what looked like a surefire double-play ball, and it seemed to everyone as if the Blue Jays would get out of the bases-loaded jam. Henderson, however, got a great jump and reached second base so quickly he caused the infielder to throw the ball away. His hustle not only broke up the double play, but it allowed two runs to score. The A's went on to win the game 7-3. Henderson had reached base three times without getting a hit. Moreover, he thoroughly disrupted the Blue Jays with his running game. As Toronto and the rest of the baseball world would soon find out, Henderson was just getting started.

In Game 2, Henderson reached base four times in four appearances at the plate with two hits and two walks. After both of his walks, he took off and stole second base and then third base. The Blue Jays could not stop him, and the A's won the game, 6-3. In the first two games of the series, Henderson had two hits, four walks, and six steals. More important, the A's had come away with two victories and were just two wins away from returning to the World Series. With the championship series moving to Toronto, the Blue Jays needed to grab some momentum in their home stadium, and that is what they did in Game 3. Toronto won the game, though the Blue Jays still could not contain Henderson, who hit a double, scored two runs, and stole another base. In Game 4, Henderson blasted two home runs off Blue Jays starter Mike Flanagan to single-handedly swing the momentum back in favor of the A's. After four games, the A's had a commanding three-games-to-one lead in the series.

In his first at-bat in Game 5, Henderson walked and stole second to set up the game's first run. Toronto had not even had its first at-bat and already the team was down by a run. In his next at-bat, Henderson ripped a triple to drive in another run. The A's led 4-0 after seven innings. The Blue Jays' bats finally came to life to make the game interesting in the late innings, but Oakland was able to hold on to win the game and advance to the World Series. Henderson had been unstoppable in the American League Championship Series. In the five-game series, he hit .400, had two home runs and a triple, walked seven times, had five RBIs, and stole eight bases. Beyond the box score, Henderson thoroughly disrupted the Blue Jays with his aggressiveness at the plate and on the bases.

Toronto outfielder Lloyd Moseby had played with Henderson when the two players grew up together in Oakland, and he was very familiar with Henderson's game. After the series, Moseby said, "Rickey hasn't changed since he was a little kid. . . . He could strut before he could walk, and he always lived for the lights. When he was 10, we used to say, 'Don't let Rickey get to you because that's his game.' Twenty years later, I'm telling my teammates the same thing. But it didn't do much good." Henderson was named the MVP of the championship series for putting on one of the most impressive one-man performances in play-off history. After 11 seasons in the big leagues, Henderson was finally on his way to his first World Series.

AN UNFORGETTABLE WORLD SERIES

The 1989 World Series marked the first time that the two teams from the San Francisco Bay Area would meet to decide baseball's ultimate champion. Of the two franchises, the A's have been the most successful in World Series victories. Before 1989, the A's had won eight World Series titles in franchise history, including three straight from 1972 to 1974, as well as five championships when the team was based in Philadelphia. The Giants, on the other hand, had won five championships when the team was based in New York. Since moving to San Francisco in 1958, however, the Giants had not won any World Series titles. In fact, before 1989, they had only been in one other World Series. That series, in 1962, ended in heartbreaking fashion for the Giants in the ninth inning of the seventh game when Willie McCovey lined out extremely hard to preserve a 1-0 victory for the New York Yankees.

The first two games of the 1989 World Series were played in Oakland. Henderson picked up where he left off in the

Rickey Henderson connected on a pitch at the Oakland Coliseum during the 1989 World Series against the San Francisco Giants. Henderson batted .474 in the Series, which Oakland won in four games. The victory was Henderson's first World Series win.

American League Championship Series. In Game 1, he had two hits and drove in a run to contribute to a balanced attack by the A's, who scored five runs in the first four innings. That was more than enough run support for Oakland ace Dave Stewart, who pitched a masterful five-hit, complete-game shutout. In Game 2, Oakland's pitching again shut down the Giants. This time, it was Mike Moore and two Oakland relievers who kept the Giants in check as the A's won 5-1. Henderson ignited Oakland's attack early by leading off with a walk and stealing second base. He scored the game's first run in the bottom of the first inning on Carney Lansford's double. He finished the game with three hits in three at-bats and one stolen base. In the first two games of his first World

☆ ☆ ☆ ☆ ☆

THE DAY THE EARTH SHOOK

The San Francisco Bay Area is in a region known for earthquakes. Most of the area's quakes are minor tremors that cause a split-second jolt and rarely result in any damage. On October 17, 1989, however, the area was hit by a massive quake with an epicenter near Loma Prieta, about 50 miles (80 kilometers) south of San Francisco. Measuring 7.1 on the Richter Scale, the Loma Prieta quake ripped and rumbled through miles of earth to cause death and destruction in Northern California. Not since the famous 1906 earthquake and fire destroyed much of San Francisco had the area been hit by a disaster so devastating.

The Loma Prieta earthquake struck just after 5 P.M., about 30 minutes before the start of Game 3 of the World Series. It quickly became clear that the World Series would not be played that day. Major damage to the Bay Area included the collapse of a section of the San Francisco-Oakland Bay Bridge, the flattening of a major double-decker section of freeway in Oakland, and a blazing fire in San Francisco's Marina District. Besides causing widespread destruction and a power loss that would last for days, the earthquake resulted in thousands of injuries and more than 60 deaths. When the World Series resumed, the teams first paid tribute to the many emergency-services and rescue workers during a pregame ceremony at Candlestick Park.

Series, Henderson had erupted for five hits in eight at-bats to propel Oakland to a two-games-to-none Series lead. It was time for the "Bay Bridge Series" to cross over to the other side of the Bay to Candlestick Park in San Francisco.

Game 3 of the World Series was scheduled for October 17, 1989. About 30 minutes before game time, the teams were making their final preparations when a major earthquake struck the San Francisco Bay Area. Candlestick Park shook and swayed, but it withstood the massive tremor. When the shaking stopped, fans in the stadium chanted for the game to go on. Soon afterward, however, reports of death and destruction made it clear that the game would have to be canceled. Suddenly, baseball was the last thing on anyone's mind. In the days after the earthquake, officials from Major League Baseball and the two teams met with civic leaders to decide how to proceed. Some people felt that the World Series should be canceled altogether out of respect for the victims and their families. Others felt that it was more important to play the games and help the people of the Bay Area take their minds off of the earthquake. Baseball Commissioner Fay Vincent eventually announced that the World Series would continue after a 10-day delay.

On October 27, the Giants and the A's returned to Candlestick Park. The Giants finally put some runs on the board, but their pitching could not stop the potent A's attack. Oakland rolled to a 13-7 victory to take a three-games-to-none lead. Henderson contributed to the Game 3 explosion with a double, a walk, and two steals. The next day, the Giants came to the ballpark knowing that they were in a must-win situation. The A's, on the other hand, wanted to complete a Series sweep and keep the Giants from having any chance for a comeback. Henderson stomped on the Giants' hopes immediately by leading off the game with a home run. In the second inning, the A's continued to slam

Oakland players *(from left)* Rickey Henderson, Dennis Eckersley, and Carney Lansford appeared with the World Series trophy at a ceremony to honor the A's held on October 31, 1989, at Jack London Square in Oakland. "This means we got all the bragging rights to the Bay Area," Henderson said in one interview.

the door shut on the Giants by adding three more runs. Oakland went on to win Game 4 by a score of 9-6 to sweep the "Earthquake Series." Henderson had three more hits in the final game, plus he scored twice and drove in two RBIs. In the four-game series, Henderson hit .474 and set the tone for the Athletics' high-powered offense with his aggressive style of play. Although Henderson's performance in the World Series was definitely worthy of MVP consideration, the voters chose another deserving recipient. The award went to Henderson's teammate and fellow Oakland native Dave Stewart, who pitched the A's to victory in two of the World Series games.

Henderson may not have won the MVP award, but he did win the championship ring he had desired. And he helped to bring some cheer to his hometown. "This means we got all the bragging rights to the Bay Area. *All* the bragging rights," Henderson said in the *Boston Globe*. "I don't think Oakland is ever going to get enough credit. . . . It's just a big city on the other side of the Bay, a second city, but not in baseball."

Most Valuable Player

Rickey Henderson was a free agent after the 1989 season. He could have moved to any team but decided to stay with Oakland and signed a four-year, $12 million contract. The A's had a great team and their overriding goal was to get back to the World Series for the third straight year and win it for the second year in a row. In addition, Henderson had another goal for 1990. After coming very close in two previous years (second in 1981 and third in 1985), Henderson was determined more than ever to win the American League Most Valuable Player award. He wanted to put together the kind of season that would leave no doubt in the minds of the voters that he should be the MVP.

Henderson started off very hot right out of spring training and never faltered. In 1990, he hit for the highest

Advancing to second base, Rickey Henderson leaped over a ball hit by Carney Lansford during Game 2 of the 1990 World Series against the Cincinnati Reds. Henderson was named the American League Most Valuable Player for his performance during the 1990 season.

batting average of his career (.325). In fact, he almost won the American League batting crown, coming in second behind George Brett of the Kansas City Royals, who hit .329. In addition, Henderson hit 28 home runs and finished second in the league in slugging percentage, which was a remarkable achievement for a leadoff hitter. Henderson also led the league in on-base percentage, stolen bases, and runs scored. To make matters even better, the A's won 103 games, taking their division by nine games over the Chicago White Sox. Henderson had definitely delivered an MVP-worthy performance, and this time the voters agreed.

Henderson beat out Detroit Tigers slugger Cecil Fielder to win the award. The final voting showed that Henderson was not the only Oakland player to have an outstanding year. The A's placed six players in the top twelve in the MVP voting: relief

★ ★ ★ ★ ★
PITCHING SUPERSTARS OF THE OAKLAND A's

The Oakland team that played in three straight World Series from 1988 to 1990 dominated the American League with a fearsome batting order, but it also had a great pitching staff. Dave Stewart and Dennis Eckersley were two of the key contributors to Oakland's pitching success.

- ACE OF THE OAKLAND A'S. Dave Stewart debuted in the major leagues with the Los Angeles Dodgers in 1978, but his career did not really take off until the A's signed him in 1986. In the 1987 season, Stewart struck out 205 batters and led the American League with 20 wins. That started an impressive string of four straight years in which the Oakland ace won 20 or more games. In each of these seasons, Stewart received consideration for the Cy Young Award, but he never won the prestigious honor. The closest he came was in 1989, when he finished in second place. That same year he went 4–0 in the postseason and was named the Most Valuable Player in the World Series for his pitching dominance against the San Francisco Giants. Stewart's many memorable accomplishments include a perfect 8–0 record as a starter in American League Championship Series games, a no-hitter in 1990, and an impressive 7–1 record in head-to-head match-ups with Roger Clemens. As for his relationship with Rickey pitcher Dennis Eckersley (sixth place), starting pitcher Dave Stewart (eighth), starting pitcher Bob Welch (ninth), and sluggers Mark McGwire (eleventh) and José Canseco (twelfth).

After such a dominant season, the Oakland A's were clearly the team to beat going into the play-offs. Oakland got off to a strong start by pounding Roger Clemens and the Boston Red Sox in four straight games to win the American League

☆ ☆ ☆ ☆ ☆ ☆

Henderson, Dave Stewart said, "He was the best teammate I've ever had."

- **CLOSER SUPREME.** Dennis Eckersley broke into the major leagues in 1975. He began his career as a starting pitcher for the Cleveland Indians before moving on to the Boston Red Sox and the Chicago Cubs. Eckersley's highlights as a starter include winning the Rookie Pitcher of the Year Award in 1975, throwing a no-hitter in 1977, and winning 20 games in 1978. In 1987, the Cubs traded Eckersley to the Oakland Athletics. The A's planned to use Eckersley in the bullpen as one of their set-up relievers. When their closer became injured, "Eck" moved into that role and became one of the best of all time. Eckersley was elected to the Hall of Fame in 2004. His plaque at Cooperstown reads: "A top starting pitcher early in his career who became a dominant closer, combined a blazing fastball and devastating slider, pinpoint control, and a deceptive sidearm delivery to save 390 games. From 1988–1993, struck out 458 while walking 51. His Oakland Athletics teams appeared in three consecutive World Series from 1988–1990, winning in 1989. Won American League MVP and Cy Young awards in 1992. As starter, completed 100 games and pitched a no-hitter for Cleveland in 1977. Elected to six All-Star teams."

Championship Series. When the World Series started, the A's were in the familiar position of being the team favored to win. Unfortunately, they ran into a red-hot Cincinnati Reds team. Just as the Dodgers had done two years earlier, the Reds put together the perfect combination of great pitching and clutch hitting to send the Oakland A's to their second disappointing World Series loss in three years. Henderson had a good World Series, batting .333 and stealing three bases in four games, but it was not enough to keep the underdog Reds from providing a bitter end to what had otherwise been an excellent year for Henderson and the A's.

THE GREATEST OF ALL TIME

Henderson's MVP season in 1990 featured many great highlights, but one of the biggest moments came when Henderson passed the legendary Ty Cobb as the American League's all-time stolen-base leader. Cobb retired from baseball in 1928 with 892 stolen bases, an American League record that stood for 62 years until Henderson broke it on May 29, 1990. After passing Cobb in the record books, Henderson then set his sights on Lou Brock's major-league record of 938 steals. When the 1991 season started, Henderson only needed three steals to break Brock's record. Normally, he would have been able to steal three bases in a handful of games, if not in a single game. In 1991, however, Henderson got off to a slow start because of a contract dispute, injuries, and another controversy about whether he was really hurt. It ultimately took him about three weeks to get in position to become the all-time stolen-base champion.

On May 1, 1991, the A's were taking on the New York Yankees at the Oakland Coliseum. With Henderson taking his lead off second base, everyone in the stadium knew what was at stake. The Oakland fans had come to witness history, and that was what they saw when Henderson stole third base. Finally, he was Major League Baseball's stolen-base king. Henderson celebrated the accomplishment by pulling the base out of the ground and lifting it high above his head. The Oakland fans cheered wildly for their hometown hero as he received congratulations from his teammates, his manager, Tony La Russa, his mother, Bobbie, and others. Lou Brock was also on hand to graciously congratulate the man who broke his record. While chasing the record, Henderson had given away some of his

★ ★ ★ ★ ★

TOP 20 CAREER BASE STEALERS

Name	Years Played	Stolen Bases
Rickey Henderson	1979–2003	1,406
Lou Brock	1961–1979	938
Billy Hamilton	1888–1901	912
Ty Cobb	1905–1928	892
Tim Raines	1979–2002	808
Vince Coleman	1985–1997	752
Eddie Collins	1906–1930	744
Arlie Latham	1880–1909	739
Max Carey	1910–1929	738
Honus Wagner	1897–1917	722
Joe Morgan	1963–1984	689
Willie Wilson	1976–1994	668
Tom Brown	1882–1898	657
Bert Campaneris	1964–1983	649
Kenny Lofton	1991–present	622
Otis Nixon	1983–1999	620
George Davis	1890–1909	616
Dummy Hoy	1888–1902	594
Maury Wills	1959–1972	586
George Van Haltren	1887–1903	583

Rickey Henderson slid headfirst to steal third base during a game on May 1, 1991, against the New York Yankees. The stolen base, which was Henderson's 939th, broke Lou Brock's career record. Henderson's comments after breaking the record led to some criticism in the media.

earlier stolen bases as special gifts to people who helped him in his career. For example, after stealing his 893rd base to break Cobb's American League record, Henderson presented the base to his minor-league manager Tom Trebelhorn. Likewise, when he stole base 938 to tie Brock's record, Henderson gave the base to A's owner Walter Haas. Now, after finally breaking the all-time record, Henderson stood with the base in his hands—this was one stolen base he would keep for himself.

Although Henderson's record-breaking achievement was truly remarkable, the day did not pass without controversy.

During the celebration, Henderson made a speech to the crowd. He thanked many people, including the A's owners and organization, the city of Oakland, the fans, his mother, his family, friends, and former managers Tom Trebelhorn and Billy Martin. Henderson then wrapped up his speech by saying, "Lou Brock was the symbol of great base stealing. But today, I'm the greatest of all time." Some people took offense to these words, saying that Henderson was a selfish and egotistical superstar for calling himself "the greatest of all time." Henderson, however, felt that he was just being honest and did not mean to be disrespectful to Brock. Still, he could not take back the words, and the media turned his remarks into a big controversy. Moreover, on the same day that Henderson broke the all-time steals record, pitching great Nolan Ryan threw his seventh no-hitter. Many in the media used this turn of events to point out how humble and respectful Ryan was compared with Henderson. Still, while some people would criticize Henderson's speech that day, no one could deny that he had done something spectacular.

In a 2003 interview in *Baseball Digest*, Henderson said that he was trying to pay respect to boxer Muhammad Ali, who used the phrase, "I'm the greatest." Henderson added that Brock had helped him write what he was going to say and had no problem with the line. "As soon as I said it, it ruined everything," Henderson said. "Everybody thought it was the worst thing you could ever say. Those words haunt me to this day."

As it would turn out, Henderson's pursuit of Brock's record would be one of the few highlights for the A's in what was otherwise a disappointing season. After three straight trips to the World Series, the A's fell all the way to fourth place in the division.

The A's bounced back strong in 1992, winning 96 games to retake the American League West. Oakland's rise back to the top featured a familiar blend of offensive firepower and superb pitching. Henderson also played well and continued to add to his stolen-base record. Exactly one year after breaking Brock's stolen-base record, Henderson became the first player in history to steal 1,000 bases. Returning to the play-offs, the A's squared off against the Toronto Blue Jays. Three years earlier, Henderson had been a one-man wrecking crew in the Athletics' American League Championship Series victory over Toronto. This time, the Blue Jays turned the tables on the A's by beating Oakland in six games on their way to capturing their first-ever World Series championship. In the four seasons since reacquiring Henderson from the Yankees, the A's had been one of baseball's most dominant teams. This play-off loss to Toronto, however, signaled the end to this era of excellence for the Oakland franchise.

A HIRED GUN

The 1993 season turned into a nightmare for the A's. After nearly reaching the World Series the previous year, Oakland finished dead last in its division. Many of the players who had contributed to the Athletics' run of greatness were gone, including José Canseco, Carney Lansford, Walt Weiss, and Dave Stewart. In late July, Henderson joined the list of departed players when he was traded to the Toronto Blue Jays for pitcher Steve Karsay and a player to be named later. Four years earlier, the A's had picked up Henderson from the Yankees to help ignite their offense and improve their shot at winning it all. Now, the Blue Jays were in the same position. They wanted Henderson to provide a spark that would help them win their second straight World Series.

At the time of the trade, Henderson was playing great for the A's. He was hitting .327 and leading the team in many offensive categories, including runs scored, steals, walks, and home runs. Though he did not put up the same kind of numbers with Toronto, batting only .215 in 44 games, Henderson nevertheless helped the team achieve its goal of making it back to the play-offs.

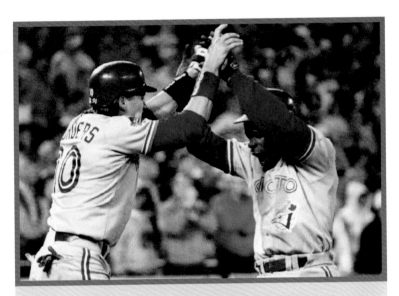

Crossing home plate, Rickey Henderson high-fived Pat Borders during Game 4 of the 1993 World Series. Henderson scored the game-winning run for Toronto, which went on to defeat the Philadelphia Phillies in the Series.

The Blue Jays beat the Chicago White Sox in the American League Championship Series to earn the right to play the Philadelphia Phillies in the World Series. Compared with his previous trips to the play-offs, Henderson did not have a great postseason. He did, however, play a part in one of the most memorable moments in World Series history. With Toronto trailing in Game 6 by the score of 6-5, Henderson led off the ninth inning with a walk. One out later, he moved over to second base on Paul Molitor's single. That brought Toronto slugger Joe Carter to the plate to face Phillies closer Mitch "Wild Thing" Williams. Everyone knew that Henderson would be off and running on any hit and would do anything to try to score the tying run. As it turned out, he did not have to run hard. After working the count to two balls and two strikes, Carter blasted a three-run homer that won the game and the World Series for the Blue Jays.

Carter's ninth-inning blast stands as the only come-from-behind, Series-ending home run in the history of the Fall Classic.

At the end of the season, Henderson was once again a free agent. He could have signed with Toronto or with any other team. Instead, he chose to return to a familiar location. On December 17, 1993, Henderson reached an agreement to return home by signing a two-year deal with the Oakland A's worth $8.5 million. "I didn't have any bad feelings about the organization," Henderson said in an interview during spring training in 1994. "I've had success all my career here. . . . I hope I can go out and perform to my capabilities."

Chasing
History

When Rickey Henderson returned to Oakland for the 1994 season, the team was looking to rebound from a last-place finish the previous year. Sure enough, the Oakland club made a bit of a comeback in 1994. The team had a record of 51–63 but was in second place in the moribund American League West, a game behind the Texas Rangers, when a strike by the players ended the season on August 12. The strike, mainly over the team owners' wish for a salary cap, lasted into the early part of the following season and led to the cancellation of the 1994 World Series. Henderson was slowed by injury and only appeared in 87 of Oakland's 114 games in 1994. Still, he was among the league leaders in walks and on-base percentage. He also continued to climb the ranks of the all-time leaders in walks and runs scored. In addition, Henderson kept adding to his stolen-base record and finished the season with 1,117 stolen bases for his career.

In 1995, Henderson bounced back to play in 112 games and have a productive year. He led the A's with a .300 average, stole 32 bases, scored 67 runs, and drove in 54 RBIs. With many critics counting him out as too old—he was now 36—and too injury-prone at this stage of his career, Henderson proved he could still be a force on the field. He also continued to build on his many franchise records with the A's. Even though he had spent four and a half seasons in the prime of his career with the Yankees, Henderson was now the Oakland Athletics' franchise leader in many important categories, "including games (1,552), at-bats (5,598), runs (1,169), hits (1,640), doubles (273), triples (40), walks (1,109), total bases (2,452), steals (801), batting (.293) and on-base percentage (.412)," according to Henderson's entry on *The Baseball Page* Web site. Although Henderson put up good numbers for the A's in 1995, the team slumped to last place in the division. After the season, Henderson's two-year contract was up, and he signed as a free agent with the San Diego Padres. For the first time in his baseball career, he was going to play in the National League.

"It gave me an opportunity to start fresh and learn from one of the greatest hitters," said Henderson about the deal, referring to six-time National League batting champion Tony Gwynn. The two-year contract with the Padres was worth $4 million, with about $2.5 million more in incentives based on plate appearances.

RICKEY ON THE MOVE

In his first year in the National League, Henderson had a good season with the Padres. Although he did not hit for a high average (.241), he maintained a high on-base percentage by walking 125 times. In addition, he was still a threat to run whenever he reached base. He finished the year with 37 stolen bases. He also

Now with the San Diego Padres, Rickey Henderson hit a solo home run in the sixth inning of Game 1 of the 1996 National League Division Series against the St. Louis Cardinals. Henderson batted .333 in the series, but the Cardinals swept the Padres.

finished second on the team with 110 runs scored. Henderson provided the flash for a powerful Padres lineup that featured hard-hitting MVP third baseman Ken Caminiti, slugging center fielder Steve Finley, and sweet-swinging Tony Gwynn, one of the best hitters of all time. San Diego won the National League West. Back in the play-off spotlight, Henderson elevated his game in the Division Series against the St. Louis Cardinals. He started the series off right for the Padres by hitting a home run in Game 1, and he ended up batting .333 for the series. Unfortunately, his play was not enough to keep the Cardinals from sweeping the series and putting an end to San Diego's season.

In 1997, the Padres could not repeat their success and fell to fourth place in the National League West. Looking to rebuild, San Diego traded Henderson in midseason to the Anaheim Angels for pitchers Ryan Hancock and Steven Agosto and a player to be named later. The Angels wanted Henderson to give them a boost for their play-off run, but their plans were not realized. Before the trade, Henderson had been hitting .274 and having a productive year for San Diego. In Anaheim, however, he never found his groove. He slumped badly and only hit .183 in 32 games for the Angels, who finished the season in second place in the American League West behind the Seattle Mariners. Though Henderson did not hit well for Anaheim, he was as effective as ever on the base paths, stealing 16 bases in 20 attempts. At this stage in his career, he was not stealing as many bases as he did when he was younger, but he still had an excellent stolen-base percentage. For the combined 1997 season with San Diego and Anaheim, Henderson stole 45 bases in 53 attempts. After the season, he returned once again to the Oakland A's as a free agent.

"It's no secret that Rickey has seen much of his success with the Oakland Athletics. He's very excited to be returning to the team," his agent, Jeff Borris, told The Associated Press after the one-year deal was completed.

In 1998, Rickey Henderson was back in Oakland for his fourth stint with the A's. Here, he keeps his eye on the pitcher while taking a large lead off first base. At age 39, Henderson led the American League in stolen bases—the oldest player ever to do so.

When Henderson rejoined the A's in 1998, it was his fourth time in Oakland and his twentieth season in the major leagues. Even at his age and with all the wear and tear of running and sliding for so many years, Henderson was still one of the game's top base stealers. He had not led the league in steals since 1991, but he was still consistently among the league leaders. In 1998, however, the 39-year-old "Man of Steal" turned back the clock and once again soared to the very top of the leaderboard. Henderson stole 66 bases for the season on his way to becoming the oldest player ever to lead the league in steals. It was also the twelfth season he had been the league leader in stolen bases. Henderson demonstrated his durability by playing in 152 games for the season, which was his highest total since 1986 and the third-highest total of his career. He further proved how productive he could be by

☆ ☆ ☆ ☆ ☆

THE PERFECT LEADOFF HITTER

Rickey Henderson is generally considered one of the greatest leadoff hitters of all time—if not the greatest. Here are some of the aspects of Henderson's game that made him the premier leadoff hitter of his or any other era.

- ON-BASE PERCENTAGE. The main goal of the leadoff hitter is to get on base so he can score runs. Henderson was the ideal leadoff man because he was a good hitter and he had a great eye. In his 25 years in the majors, Henderson ranked in the top 10 in on-base percentage 16 times (and was in the top five 12 times).

- SPEED. In general, leadoff hitters are players who can use their speed to get around the bases and score runs. Henderson used his tremendous speed to beat out infield hits, steal bases, break up double plays, and take extra bases whenever possible.

- DISRUPTIVE FORCE. Henderson was a disruptive force whenever he reached base. Every time he got on base, he made the other team worry about what he was going to do next. The more the other team worried about Henderson, the less attention they paid to other things, such as the hitter standing at the plate.

- POWER STROKE. Leadoff hitters are typically not power hitters. Henderson, however, was an exception. He could leading the A's with 118 walks and 101 runs scored. It was a remarkable performance for anyone, let alone for a player who was nearly 40 years old.

"He can still get on base, and he can still score runs. And he's the best I've ever seen at working a count and making a pitcher work every ounce," said Art Howe, the manager of the A's.

☆ ☆ ☆ ☆ ☆ ☆

definitely hit the long ball. Henderson finished his career with nearly 300 home runs and set a record with 81 homers to lead off a game.

- **THE REST OF THE LINEUP.** The job of the leadoff man is to get on base, but it's equally important for him to have teammates who can move him around the bases and drive him home. In particular, Henderson relied heavily on the second hitter in the lineup to move him, either by getting a hit, sacrificing him to the next base, or taking pitches to give him more opportunities to steal. Henderson also relied on good RBI hitters in the heart of the order to drive him home.

Billy Martin, who managed Henderson for the A's and the Yankees, knew his value as a leadoff hitter. According to Martin, Henderson "has to be the greatest leadoff man in the history of baseball. There has never been a leadoff man like him, not with his power and speed. . . . How many leadoff men do you know who can bat .314, get 172 hits, score 146 runs, hit 24 homers, drive in 72 runs, get 99 walks, and steal 80 bases? Only one. Rickey Henderson. And that's exactly what he did for the Yankees in 1985. . . . That's why I say he's the greatest leadoff man in baseball history and the best player in the game today."

After his excellent season in Oakland, Henderson was on the move again in 1999. This time he signed with the New York Mets, hoping for a chance to win another title. "I've never lost my desire," he said during a news conference announcing his signing with the Mets. "I still love the game. I don't think anything is left now in this game for me but to be a winner. The best thing is to be a winner. The worst thing is losing."

Henderson played in 121 games for the Mets, hitting for a .315 average and helping the team earn the wild-card spot in the National League play-offs. He had an excellent series against the Arizona Diamondbacks in the National League Division Series. He hit .400 and swiped six bases, a record for a division series, to help the Mets beat the Diamondbacks, three games to one. That set up what turned out to be a very memorable matchup with the Atlanta Braves in the National League Championship Series. The Mets fell into a deep hole by losing the first three games of the series. After taking Game 4, New York then rallied dramatically to win the next game by scoring two runs in the bottom of the fifteenth inning. Game 6 turned out to be another extra-inning nail-biter. After the Mets scored a run in the top of the tenth inning to take the lead, the Braves stayed alive by tying the game in the bottom of the inning. In the following inning, the Braves scored another run to win the game and earn a trip to the World Series.

Although Henderson had a good season for the Mets and a great play-off series against the Diamondbacks, he ran into problems during the championship series against the Braves. The trouble started in Game 4 (the first Mets victory of the series) when Henderson was pulled out of the game in the eighth inning after he had already taken his place in the outfield. Henderson was upset by the way he was taken out of the game. As it turned out, Mets manager Bobby Valentine later admitted that he forgot to tell Henderson that he was coming out for defensive purposes. As that controversy began to subside, another one exploded when reports surfaced that Henderson and Bobby Bonilla were playing cards in the clubhouse while the Mets were trying to beat the Braves in Game 6. The media and the fans blasted Henderson for being a selfish player who cared about himself more than he cared about the team.

The bitterness from this controversy lingered after the season. Moreover, things did not get any better in 2000, and the Mets released Henderson after 31 games. Within days of his release, the Seattle Mariners snatched up Henderson. He introduced himself to his new team with a bang by leading off his first two games with home runs. Henderson played in 92 games for the Mariners and helped the team reach the playoffs, where they beat the Chicago White Sox in the first round before falling to the Yankees in six games in the championship series. While playing for Seattle, Henderson continued his assault on two impressive major-league records. On May 23, 2000, Henderson walked for the 2,000th time in his career to become only the third player at the time to accomplish this feat (the other two were Babe Ruth and Ted Williams). In addition, Henderson continued to climb higher on the list of one of baseball's most important records by moving into second place behind Ty Cobb for the most runs scored. Indeed, Henderson was in elite company.

THE YEAR OF MAJOR MILESTONES

Henderson returned to the San Diego Padres in 2001. In order to make sure he was ready for the season, Henderson began the year with the Padres' Class AAA team in Portland. He was soon called up to the big leagues when two Padre outfielders were injured. Once he was back in the majors, it did not take long for Henderson to achieve his next major career milestone. On April 25, 2001, in a game against the Philadelphia Phillies, Henderson drew a base on balls to pass Babe Ruth as the all-time walks leader. Henderson then set his sights on Cobb's record for most runs scored. Henderson nudged toward the record as the season progressed, and he tied it on October 3, 2001. A

Fans in San Diego cheered as Rickey Henderson ran down the third-base line to score the 2,247th run of his career on October 4, 2001. The run broke the all-time record held by Ty Cobb.

day later, Henderson stepped up to bat against the Los Angeles Dodgers and quickly ended the suspense by hitting a home run. As his ecstatic teammates gathered around home plate to congratulate him, Henderson trotted around the bases. Before they could mob him at the plate, Henderson motioned for everyone to clear a path. He wanted to do something special to celebrate in style and make the moment even more memorable, so at the end of his home-run trot Henderson slid home. He was now alone as the major-league leader for most runs scored. To mark the occasion, Tony Gwynn presented Henderson with a gold-plated home plate.

☆ ☆ ☆ ☆ ☆ ☆

CAREER LEADERS IN RUNS

Name	Years Played	Runs
Rickey Henderson	1979–2003	2,295
Ty Cobb	1905–1928	2,246
Barry Bonds	1986–present	2,227
Hank Aaron	1954–1976	2,174
Babe Ruth	1914–1935	2,174
Pete Rose	1963–1986	2,165
Willie Mays	1951–1973	2,062
Cap Anson	1871–1897	1,996
Stan Musial	1941–1963	1,949
Lou Gehrig	1923–1939	1,888
Tris Speaker	1907–1928	1,882
Mel Ott	1926–1947	1,859
Craig Biggio	1988–2007	1,844
Frank Robinson	1956–1976	1,829
Eddie Collins	1906–1930	1,821
Carl Yastrzemski	1961–1983	1,816
Ted Williams	1939–1960	1,798
Paul Molitor	1978–1998	1,782
Charlie Gehringer	1924–1942	1,774
Jimmie Foxx	1925–1945	1,751

"Going out and scoring so many runs is not just an individual record," Henderson said in a news conference after the game. "It's a record that you've got to have your teammates help you out, and in the 23 years, I've had some great teammates."

A few days later, in the final game of the year, Henderson added another highlight to his memorable season. Just one shy of the 3,000-hit club, Henderson stepped up to the plate against the Colorado Rockies and quickly flared a double into the outfield. It was not the hardest ball he ever hit, but that did not matter. Standing on second base, Henderson had become only the twenty-fifth player in major-league history to reach the 3,000-hit plateau.

The day was special in more ways than one for the San Diego organization and all of the fans in attendance. Not only did they see Henderson's 3,000th hit, but they were also on hand to see the last game in the Hall of Fame career of Tony Gwynn, the greatest player in the history of the franchise. Before the game, Henderson offered to sit out so that he would not take any of the spotlight away from the Padre legend, but Gwynn told Henderson to play and go for his 3,000th hit. After the game, Henderson said about his milestone hit, "It's a great feeling, a feeling you can't really describe. I thought I would never get there because I walk so much. If you continue to play as long as I've been playing, you get the opportunity to do it."

Henderson was on the move again at the end of the year. In 2002, he signed on with the Boston Red Sox but appeared in only 72 games. The following year, he was unable to land a job on a major-league team at the start of the season, so he signed a contract to play with the Newark Bears of the independent Atlantic League of Professional Baseball. At this point in his career, many people wondered why Henderson would still play when he was not wanted by any major-league teams. Never one to pay attention to the critics, Henderson continued to play for the love of the game and for another shot in the major leagues, even if it was a long shot. Regardless of his age, Henderson was determined to prove the critics wrong and show everyone that he still had the skills to help a major-league club. "I still enjoy the game," he told the *New York*

★ ★ ★ ★ ★ ★
TONY GWYNN:
HALL OF FAME TEAMMATE

Tony Gwynn played his entire career—nearly 20 years—with the San Diego Padres. One of the best hitters of all time, Gwynn won eight batting titles, appeared in 15 All-Star Games, earned seven Silver Slugger awards, and had a career batting average of .338. He was elected to the Baseball Hall of Fame in 2007, his first year of eligibility. Gwynn was selected on 532 out of 545 ballots, the seventh-highest percentage in Hall of Fame voting history. Besides being a great player, Gwynn was one of the classiest individuals ever to play the game. Rickey Henderson and Tony Gywnn crossed paths twice during their careers, playing together on the Padres in 1996 and 1997, and again in 2001.

Though Henderson was often criticized for being a hot dog, he also received support over the years from many of his teammates. During the 2001 season, for example, Gwynn had the following praise for Henderson. "To me, Rickey has done more in this game than just about anybody who has played it, with the exception of Hank Aaron and maybe Pete Rose to a certain degree. At the end of this season, he could be the all-time leader in three categories, and that just doesn't happen. . . . The negative stuff that people were talking about when we got him here . . . I haven't seen it. . . . I've seen a guy who's prepared, I've seen a guy who works hard, who loves to help young guys and who has done whatever the club has asked him to do, not only on the field but off the field. He's been a perfect citizen as long as he's been here. That's the Rickey I know."

Rickey Henderson used a pop-up slide to beat a throw home while playing in a preseason game in May 2005 with the San Diego Surf Dawgs of the Golden Baseball League. Henderson, 46, batted .270 with the Surf Dawgs and stole 16 bases in 18 tries.

Times just before his debut with the Bears. "I plan to get back to the major leagues. This gives me an opportunity to stay in shape and get live pitching. Maybe someone in the major leagues needs help, and I can help out. I'm available." In

56 games for Newark, Henderson hit .339 with 8 home runs and 33 RBIs. His performance was good enough to earn him a spot in the league's All-Star Game, where he was named the MVP. His performance in Newark also garnered the attention of the Los Angeles Dodgers, who signed Henderson after Major League Baseball's All-Star break. Henderson started off well but suffered a shoulder injury and only played in 30 games for the Dodgers.

After the 2003 season, Henderson was once again a free agent. Unable to land a position with a major-league team, he rejoined the Newark Bears in 2004. He hit .281 for the Bears and had an impressive on-base percentage of .462. Moreover, at 45 years old, Henderson showed no signs of slowing down on the base paths. He stole 37 bases for the Bears and was caught stealing only twice. Unfortunately, he was not picked up by any major-league teams, marking the first year he had not played in the majors since 1979.

The following year, Henderson signed with the San Diego Surf Dawgs of the newly formed Golden Baseball League, another independent professional baseball organization. Again, Henderson showed that he could still play by hitting .270, having an on-base percentage of .456, and stealing 16 bases in 18 tries. His performance during these two seasons with the Newark Bears and the San Diego Surf Dawgs showed how much he still loved the game and wanted to earn another shot on a big-league roster. In addition, these two seasons demonstrated a lot about Henderson's incredible talent. Though he was not the same player that he was in his prime, he was still a productive player. Moreover, he was still an amazing base stealer. In his two seasons with the Newark Bears and the San Diego Surf Dawgs, Henderson stole 53 bases in 57 attempts. This would be an incredible achievement for any player at any level. To think that Henderson did this when he was over 45 years old is phenomenal.

On to
the Hall

There may never be a more dynamic, explosive personality on the baseball field than Rickey Henderson. He was uniquely talented, confident to the point of cockiness, and always very talkative. In fact, it's possible that he might go down in history as the most talkative player ever in the big leagues. He talked to opposing players when he was on the bases. He talked to fans while he was playing in the outfield. He talked to himself when he was in the batter's box. It has also been reported that he talked to himself in the mirror while practicing his swing before games and talked to his bats to find out which one was going to give him a hit in the game.

Henderson had his share of critics—people who thought he was nothing more than an egotistical and selfish superstar.

But even his harshest critics had to admit that Henderson was one of the most talented players in the game. A self-proclaimed hot dog, or showboat, Henderson always saw himself as an entertainer on the field. As he said, "People are paying to see you play. If you're not entertaining them, why should they watch?" As competitive as he was, Henderson always seemed to be having fun on the field, and that sense of fun could be seen in the way he played the game and in the way he interacted with his fellow ballplayers and fans. He was blessed with an incredible talent and he used that talent to entertain the fans—and to entertain himself.

As much as Henderson attracted the spotlight on the field, he has always led a relatively quiet life outside of baseball. Even at the height of his superstardom, Henderson seemed to fade out of the spotlight as soon as the season was over. And, as controversial as he could be because of what he may have said or because of his style of play, Henderson never caused any trouble away from the field. When he was not at the ballpark, Henderson liked to spend time fishing and working on his large ranch near Yosemite National Park in California, where he takes care of horses, cows, pigs, and chickens. Henderson and his wife, Pamela, who met while in high school, have three daughters, Angela, Alexis, and Adriann.

Rickey Henderson has not officially retired yet, but it is hard to imagine that he will play again. In 2006, he was offered a roster spot with the San Diego Surf Dawgs, but he decided not to join the team. It was the first season in decades that he was not running around a field somewhere stealing bases, scoring runs, and wreaking havoc on the opposition. Even though he has not played for a couple of years now, Henderson certainly has not lost any of his passion for the game. As he told a reporter in the summer of 2006: "I still love the game; I still can play the game. I just gotta get that fire burned out of me. I still have that passion to play."

With his family surrounding him, Rickey Henderson cut the ribbon on August 11, 2006, at the dedication of the Rickey Henderson Baseball Field in Oakland. With Henderson at the ceremony were *(from left)* daughter Angela; his wife, Pamela; daughter Adriann; his mother, Bobbie; and daughter Alexis.

That same summer, Henderson attended a special celebration in Oakland. He was back in his hometown to help commemorate the reopening of a renovated youth baseball field. As the special guest of honor, Henderson participated in the ribbon-cutting ceremony by throwing out the first pitch to a young player from the Oakland Babe Ruth League. It had been many years since Henderson played on

Oakland's youth-league fields. Now, the man who had once been king of Bushrod Park was standing on a beautiful new field that many young ballplayers would call their home away from home, as he had done when he was a child. Henderson spoke about the importance of the park: "This is an opportunity for the kids to come to a park that they feel safe about, and they can go out and play and have fun. . . . You never know what's going to come out of this ballpark. There may be another Rickey Henderson playing in this ballpark." He also talked about the importance of being a role model in the community. "Being able to play in Oakland and growing up in Oakland was very special to me. And now, the kids can follow in [my] footsteps, and they have the chance to become a professional athlete. This is just a great feeling." As part of the ceremony, the renovated park was getting a new name—it would now be known as the Rickey Henderson Baseball Field.

Later in 2006, Henderson threw out another ceremonial first pitch. This one was at the Oakland Coliseum, where the A's were taking on the Minnesota Twins in Game 3 of the 2006 American League Division Series. A few days earlier, Henderson and many other former Oakland players gathered at a rally to support their team. One by one, the former A's players were announced. Some of them, like Vida Blue, John "Blue Moon" Odom, Billy North, and Bert "Campy" Campaneris, had played on Oakland's dynasty of the early 1970s. Others, like Carney Lansford, Dave Henderson, Mike Moore, and Dave Stewart, had been Henderson's teammates on the 1989 World Series championship club.

The A's fans enthusiastically greeted all of their favorite ballplayers, but they saved their loudest cheers for Henderson. Even before the announcer could say his name, the familiar chant rose from the crowd, "Rickey . . . Rickey . . . Rickey." Ever the showman, Henderson flashed his trademark smile and waved to the fans. He looked as if he was having a great time. Nearly 50 years old, Henderson appeared to be in excellent shape, like he was still keeping his body ready for the next call from a big-league team. He had come to the rally to show his support for a new generation of A's players, but Henderson probably wished he could be helping the team on the field instead. As he said to a reporter at the time, "In my deep heart, I know I can compete. . . . In my own heart, I know I can still play."

★ ★ ★ ★ ★
HOMETOWN HERO: REGGIE OR RICKEY?

In 2006, Major League Baseball asked fans to vote for the player they judged to be the single greatest player in the history of each franchise. The five "Hometown Hero" nominees for the A's were Jim "Catfish" Hunter, Dennis Eckersley, Lefty Grove, Reggie Jackson, and Rickey Henderson. When the final vote was counted, the A's fans chose Jackson as their "Hometown Hero." The Hall of Fame slugger, who earned the nickname "Mr. October" for his ability to deliver in the postseason, played nine seasons for the Athletics and was a key contributor to the great Oakland dynasty of the early 1970s. Even though he had many great accomplishments with the A's, Jackson chose to be represented on his Hall of Fame plaque as a New York Yankee, where he played from 1977 to 1981. Without doubt, Jackson was one of the greatest A's players, but it is hard to choose an Oakland "Hometown Hero" more worthy than Rickey Henderson.

The accompanying chart, compiled from the Oakland Athletics Web site, compares the numbers that Henderson and Jackson put

THE KING OF STEALS STEPS INTO THE COACHING BOX

Henderson has not played in the majors since 2003, but he has still been involved in the game. In 2006, he spent some time working as a special instructor with the New York Mets. In particular, Henderson worked with Mets shortstop José Reyes to help this speedy young player become a better base stealer and a more complete ballplayer. Henderson did not rule out the possibility that he might do some more work as a coach

☆ ☆ ☆ ☆ ☆

up while they were with the A's. The number in parentheses indicates where these two superstars rank among A's franchise leaders. Who would you choose?

	Rickey Henderson	Reggie Jackson
Games	1,704 (2nd)	1,346 (11th)
At-bats	6,140 (2nd)	4,686 (12th)
Hits	1,768 (3rd)	1,228 (18th)
Doubles	289 (6th)	234 (13th)
Triples	41 (24th)	27 (40th)
Home runs	167 (12th)	269 (3rd)
Runs	1,270 (1st)	756 (12th)
RBIs	648 (16th)	776 (7th)
Walks	1,227 (1st)	633 (13th)
Stolen bases	867 (1st)	145 (11th)
On-base percentage	.409 (5th)	.355 (26th)
Slugging percentage	.430 (28th)	.496 (8th)
Batting average	.288 (21st)	.262 (59th)

Rickey Henderson became a full-time first-base coach with the New York Mets in July 2007. Here, he talks with Carlos Delgado at Shea Stadium in New York. Henderson had worked with the team as a special instructor in 2006 and earlier in 2007. "I wanted to be a coach," Henderson said. "It's my dream—outside of playing baseball."

in the future. As he said, "I did some part-time work with the Mets (as an instructor). It went well. I know I can relate to players. If I don't get a chance as a player, I can use my expertise to help out kids."

When the 2007 season began, the Mets again invited him to be a special instructor to help during spring training and part time during the season. Midway through the year, the Mets were in first place in the National League East. Though the team was at the top of the division, its players were not hitting well, so management decided to make some changes to the coaching staff. The team fired hitting coach Rick Down and announced that Henderson would join the club as a full-time coach. It was not immediately clear if Henderson would become the hitting coach or if he would join the Mets in some other capacity. Soon afterward, the Mets announced that Howard Johnson would switch from first-base coach to hitting coach and that Henderson would take over Johnson's spot as the first-base coach. Henderson was also named the team's outfield and baserunning coach.

Earlier in the year, Henderson had still talked about his dream to play again in the big leagues. However, upon taking the full-time coaching job for the Mets, he seemed another step closer to finally acknowledging that his playing days were over. Yet, in typical fashion, Henderson joked with reporters about envisioning a time in which he might come back. He said, "If it was a situation where we were going to win the World Series and I was the only player they had left, I would put on the shoes . . . I haven't submitted retirement papers to MLB, but I think MLB already had their papers that I was retired."

It has yet to be seen how these coaching changes will work out for the Mets. At first glance, however, it seems as if this is the perfect job for Henderson. Who better to help the team on the base paths than the greatest base stealer of all time? Henderson definitely has the knowledge and experience to be a great first-base coach. In addition, after working on and off for two years as a special instructor for the Mets, he knows the players, and they know him. Mets manager Willie Randolph played with Henderson for four years when they were teammates on the New York Yankees. When asked about Henderson becoming a full-time coach for the Mets, Randolph said, "We have a great relationship. . . . The players have responded to a lot of his teachings, so it will be good to have him."

Henderson may finally be resigned to the idea that he will not play again, but he still has a huge passion for the game of baseball—and for mentoring a new generation of players. As he said, "I wanted to be a coach. It's my dream—outside of playing baseball. . . . I can bring excitement. I can bring a winning feeling."

THE "WOW" FACTOR

Regardless of whether he plays again, Henderson has secured his place as one of the greatest baseball players of all time. He definitely has the numbers, awards, and championships to prove it. Beyond the statistics, however, Henderson's talent on the field thrilled the fans, drove his opponents crazy, and left his managers singing his praises. Manager Billy Martin, for example, included Henderson as one of his favorite players. When putting together his baseball dream team, Martin wrote, "One other player belongs on any list of mine. Make him my third outfielder with Mantle and Mays. I'm talking about Rickey Henderson, who I think is the most exciting and best all-around player in the game today." Tony La Russa, who managed Henderson in Oakland when the team won the 1989 World Series and Henderson captured the 1990 American League MVP, had similar praise. La Russa was asked, "Which one player during your time in baseball has taken your breath away?" He responded, "I've gasped at a lot of them, but the one who made me go 'wow' the most is Rickey. He's the most dangerous player of the era I've been involved with.'"

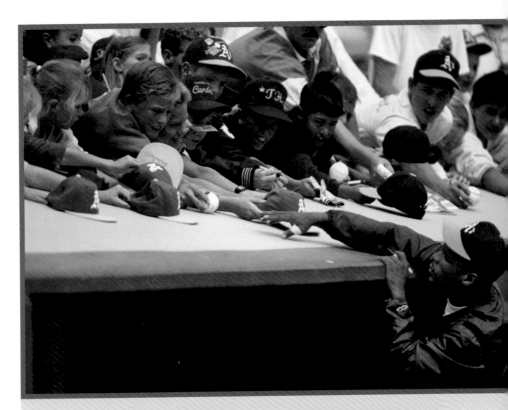

Over his lengthy career, Rickey Henderson won plenty of games and set plenty of records. He brought more than just his skills to the game, though—he also brought a sense of fun and excitement that made a connection with the fans.

One day in the not-too-distant future, Rickey Henderson will be voted into the Baseball Hall of Fame in Cooperstown, New York. His achievements are numerous—two-time World Series champion, 10-time All-Star, MVP of the American League, MVP of the American League Championship Series, more than 3,000 hits, second on the all-time walks list, and first on the list for most runs scored. And, of course, he is the undisputed stolen-base king of Major League Baseball. His record now stands at 1,406 steals, nearly 500 more than Lou Brock. It may have been a controversial statement when

★ ★ ★ ★ ★ ★
COOPERSTOWN

The National Baseball Hall of Fame and Museum is in Cooperstown, New York. It is a special place dedicated to preserving the history of the national pastime and recognizing the great players and others who made professional baseball what it is today. The Hall of Fame opened its doors on June 12, 1939, though the first players were elected in 1936. The players in the first group were Ty Cobb, Babe Ruth, Honus Wagner, Christy Mathewson, and Walter Johnson. As of the writing of this book, 280 people have been voted into the Hall of Fame, including 227 players, 17 managers, 8 umpires, and 28 other major contributors to the game.

Currently, there are two ways a player can gain entry into the Hall of Fame. They can be voted in by the Baseball Writers' Association of America (BBWAA), or they can be selected by the Veterans Committee. Each year, the BBWAA compiles a ballot featuring qualified players with 10 or more years' experience who have been retired for at least five years. To gain entry into the Hall, a player must be selected on at least 75 percent of the ballots. If a player receives 5 to 75 percent of the vote, their name is carried over to the next ballot. If they are chosen on less than 5 percent of the ballots, the player is removed from future ballots. In addition, there is a process in which the Veterans Committee looks back at players who were previously passed over and determines if they should be reconsidered for eligibility into the Hall of Fame. On rare occasions, there are exceptions to these rules for induction. In general, however, and as it should be, it is difficult to gain entry into this most hallowed shrine dedicated to baseball's greatest players.

he said it at the time, but when it comes to base stealing, Henderson is indeed "the greatest of all time." In addition to the records and awards, when Henderson enters the Hall of Fame, he will be remembered for having a style all his own. Some called it cocky and egotistical; others said it was entertaining and brought a lot of fun and excitement to the game. Although all of these are true, the most important thing to remember about Henderson is that his one-of-a-kind personality and incredible talent combined to make him one of the most exciting and productive players in the game of baseball. There will never be another player like Rickey Henderson.

STATISTICS

RICKEY HENDERSON
Primary position: Left field (Also CF)

Full Name: Rickey Nelson Henley Henderson
Born: December 25, 1958, Chicago •
Height: 5'10" Weight: 195 lbs. • Teams:
Oakland Athletics (1979–1984, 1989–1993,
1994–1995, 1998); New York Yankees
(1985–1989); Toronto Blue Jays (1993); San
Diego Padres (1996–1997, 2001); Anaheim
Angels (1997); New York Mets (1999–2000);
Seattle Mariners (2000); Boston Red Sox
(2002); Los Angeles Dodgers (2003)

☆ ☆ ☆ ☆ ☆ ☆

YEAR	TEAM	G	AB	H	HR	RBI	SB	BA
1979	OAK	89	351	96	1	26	33	.274
1980	OAK	158	591	179	9	53	100	.303
1981	OAK	108	423	135	6	35	56	.319
1982	OAK	149	536	143	10	51	130	.267
1983	OAK	145	513	150	9	48	108	.292
1984	OAK	142	502	147	16	58	66	.293
1985	NYY	143	547	172	24	72	80	.314
1986	NYY	153	608	160	28	74	87	.263
1987	NYY	95	358	104	17	37	41	.291
1988	NYY	140	554	169	6	50	93	.305
1989	NYY/OAK	150	541	148	12	57	77	.274
1990	OAK	136	489	159	28	61	65	.325

Key: OAK = Oakland Athletics; NYY = New York Yankees; TOR = Toronto Blue Jays; SDP = San Diego Padres; ANA = Anaheim Angels; NYM = New York Mets; SEA = Seattle Mariners; BOS = Boston Red Sox; LAD = Los Angeles Dodgers; G = Games; AB = At-bats; H = Hits; HR = Home runs; RBI = Runs batted in; SB = Stolen bases; BA = Batting average

☆ ☆ ☆ ☆ ☆ ☆

YEAR	TEAM	G	AB	H	HR	RBI	SB	BA
1991	OAK	134	470	126	18	57	58	.268
1992	OAK	117	396	112	15	46	48	.283
1993	OAK/TOR	134	481	139	21	59	53	.289
1994	OAK	87	296	77	6	20	22	.260
1995	OAK	112	407	122	9	54	32	.300
1996	SDP	148	465	112	9	29	37	.241
1997	SDP/ANA	120	403	100	8	34	45	.248
1998	OAK	152	542	128	14	57	66	.236
1999	NYM	121	438	138	12	42	37	.315
2000	NYM/SEA	123	420	98	4	32	36	.233
2001	SDP	123	379	86	8	42	25	.227
2002	BOS	72	179	40	5	16	8	.223
2003	LAD	30	72	15	2	5	3	.208
TOTAL		3,081	10,961	3,055	297	1,115	1,406	.279

Key: OAK = Oakland Athletics; NYY = New York Yankees; TOR = Toronto Blue Jays; SDP = San Diego Padres; ANA = Anaheim Angels; NYM = New York Mets; SEA = Seattle Mariners; BOS = Boston Red Sox; LAD = Los Angeles Dodgers; G = Games; AB = At-bats; H = Hits; HR = Home runs; RBI = Runs batted in; SB = Stolen bases; BA = Batting average

CHRONOLOGY

1958 **December 25** Born in Chicago, Illinois.

1968 Moves with his family to Oakland, California.

1976 Drafted out of high school by the Oakland Athletics in the fourth round (the ninety-sixth player chosen in the draft).

Starts his minor-league career playing Class A ball in Boise, where he hits .336 and has 29 steals.

1977 Promoted to Oakland's farm team in Modesto, California; hits .345 and leads the league with 95 steals; ties a minor-league record by stealing seven bases in one game.

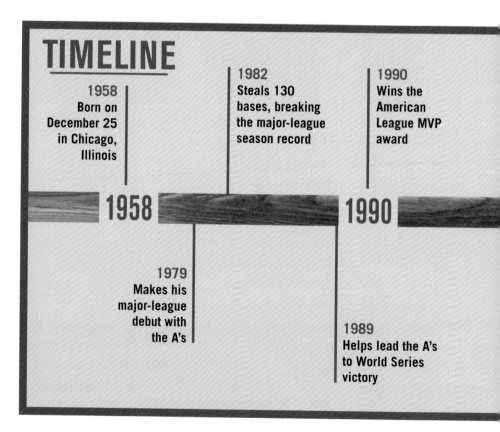

TIMELINE

1958
Born on December 25 in Chicago, Illinois

1982
Steals 130 bases, breaking the major-league season record

1990
Wins the American League MVP award

1958   1990

1979
Makes his major-league debut with the A's

1989
Helps lead the A's to World Series victory

1978   Moves up to the Class AA team in Jersey City, where he again hits over .300 and leads the league with 81 stolen bases.

1979   Begins the season at Oakland's Class AAA team in Ogden, Utah.

June 24 Is called up by the A's—in his first game, he has two hits and steals a base; plays a little more than a half-season with the A's and leads the club with 33 stolen bases.

1980   Steals 100 bases during his first full season in the major leagues, breaking Ty Cobb's old American League record of 96; earns his first trip to the All-Star Game.

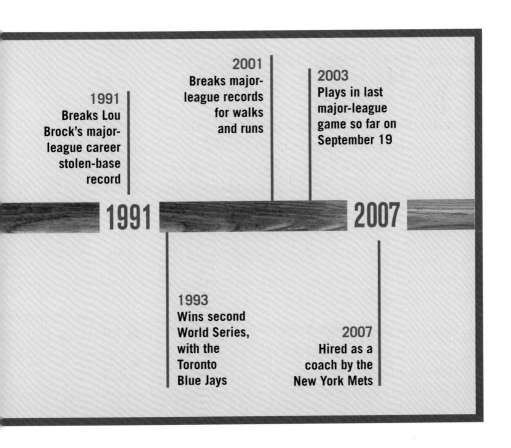

1991
Breaks Lou Brock's major-league career stolen-base record

2001
Breaks major-league records for walks and runs

2003
Plays in last major-league game so far on September 19

1991   2007

1993
Wins second World Series, with the Toronto Blue Jays

2007
Hired as a coach by the New York Mets

1981   Hits .319 for the season and leads the league in steals and hits; wins Gold Glove award for his play in the outfield and finishes second in the voting for the American League MVP behind relief pitcher Rollie Fingers of the Milwaukee Brewers.

1982   Steals 130 bases, breaking Lou Brock's former major-league record of 118 stolen bases.

1983   Steals at least 100 bases for the third time in his career.

1984   **December 5** Traded to the New York Yankees.

1985   Hits .314 with 24 home runs in his first season as a Yankee; also steals 80 bases and scores 146 runs in 143 games; finishes third in voting for the American League MVP.

1989   **June 21** Traded back to Oakland.

Is named the MVP of the American League Championship Series; helps lead the A's to victory over the San Francisco Giants in the World Series.

1990   Wins the American League MVP award after batting .325 for the season, with 119 runs, 28 home runs, 61 RBIs, and 65 steals; helps lead the A's back to the World Series, though the team loses to the underdog Cincinnati Reds.

1991   **May 1** Steals his 939th base to break Lou Brock's major-league career stolen-base record.

1992   **May 1** Becomes the first player in major-league history to steal 1,000 bases.

1993   **July 31** Traded to the Toronto Blue Jays, where he wins his second World Series.

1994   Returns as a free agent to the Oakland A's.

2001   Now playing for the San Diego Padres, breaks Babe Ruth's major-league record for walks (which has since been broken by Barry Bonds); also breaks Ty Cobb's major-league record for most runs scored; collects the 3,000th hit of his career on the last day of the season.

2003   Starts the season with the Newark Bears of the independent Atlantic League of Professional Baseball; named MVP of the league's All-Star Game; signed by the Los Angeles Dodgers after Major League Baseball's All-Star break.

September 19 Plays in what is so far his last major-league game; scores one run in the game to extend his record for runs scored to 2,295.

2004   Plays again with the Newark Bears.

2005   Signs with the San Diego Surf Dawgs of the Golden Baseball League; helps the team win the league championship.

2007   Hired by the New York Mets to be the team's first-base coach as well as its outfield and baserunning coach.

GLOSSARY

All-Star team   A team for each league, consisting of the season's best players as voted on by the fans. The All-Star Game takes place in mid-July, symbolizing the halfway point of the major-league season.

American League   One of the two leagues that are a part of Major League Baseball in the United States. The American League was established in 1900 and became a major league a year later.

assist   The official scorer awards an assist to every defensive player who fields or touches the ball (after it is hit by the batter) before a putout.

at-bat   An official turn at batting that is charged to a baseball player, except when the player walks, sacrifices, is hit by a pitched ball, or is interfered with by a catcher. At-bats are used to calculate a player's batting average and slugging percentage.

ball   A pitch that does not pass over home plate in the strike zone. A batter who receives four balls gets a walk.

batter's box   The area to the left and right of home plate in which the batter must be standing for fair play to take place.

batting average   The number of hits a batter gets divided by the number of times the player is at bat. For example, 3 hits in 10 at-bats would be a .300 batting average.

closer   A relief pitcher who is consistently used to "close" or finish the game by getting the final outs.

designated hitter   A player who bats in place of the pitcher throughout the game. (The National League does not use the designated hitter.) Since pitchers are traditionally poor hitters, the designated hitter provides more offense for a team.

disabled list   In Major League Baseball, the disabled list is a way for teams to remove injured players from their rosters.

Other players can be called up as replacements during this time.

double play   A play by the defense during which two offensive players are put out in a continuous action. A typical combination is a ground ball to the shortstop, who throws to second base to get one runner out. The second baseman then throws to the first baseman to get the batter out.

double steal   When two players steal at once; most often occurs with runners at first and third. The runner at first breaks to steal second base. When the catcher throws to second, the runner at third then breaks for home.

draft   Major League Baseball's mechanism for assigning amateur players to its teams. The draft order is determined based on the previous season's standings, with the team with the worst record receiving the first pick.

error   When a defensive player makes a mistake that results in a runner reaching base or advancing a base, an error is designated by the game's scorer.

farm team   A team that provides training and experience for young players, with the expectation that successful players will move to the major leagues.

fastball   A pitch that is thrown so that it has maximum speed. It can be gripped in any number of ways, most commonly touching two baseball seams (a two-seamer) with the index finger and middle finger, or across four seams (four-seamer). Many of today's major-league pitchers can throw more than 90 miles per hour (145 kilometers per hour).

free agent   A professional athlete who is free to negotiate a contract with any team.

hamstring   Any of three muscles at the back of the thigh that function to flex and rotate the leg and extend the thigh.

home plate   A five-sided rubber "plate" at which the batter stands to hit and which a base runner has to cross to score a run.

home run   When a batter hits a ball into the stands in fair territory, it is a home run. The batter may also hit an inside-the-park home run if the ball never leaves the playing field and the runner is able to reach home plate without being tagged by a defensive player. A home run counts as one run, and if there are any runners on base when a home run is hit, they too score.

lead   In base running, the distance a runner takes from the base toward the next base.

leadoff hitter   The first batter in the lineup.

lineup   A list that is presented to the umpire and opposing coach before the start of the game that contains the order in which the batters will bat as well as the defensive fielding positions they will play.

line drive   A batted ball, usually hit hard, that never gets too far off the ground. Typically a line drive will get beyond the infield without touching the ground, or will be hit directly at a player and be caught before it touches the ground.

MVP   The Most Valuable Player award (commonly known as the MVP) is an annual award given to one outstanding player in each league (American and National) of Major League Baseball. The award is determined by the Baseball Writers' Association of America.

minor league   Any professional league other than the major leagues.

National League   One of the two leagues that are a part of Major League Baseball in the United States. The National League was established in 1876.

pick off To put out a base runner who is off base with a quick throw, as from a pitcher or a catcher.

pinch runner A substitute base runner, often brought in during a critical situation. The pinch runner typically replaces a slower runner in the hope of stealing a base.

pitchout A pitch that is deliberately thrown out of the reach of the batter to give the catcher a better chance of throwing out a base runner.

runs batted in (RBI) The number of runs that score as a direct result of a batter's hit(s) are the runs batted in by that batter. The major-league record is 191 RBIs for a single year by one batter.

save A statistic credited to a pitcher who comes into the game with his team leading and completes the game without giving up the lead. The pitcher must be the last pitcher in the game and must fulfill at least one of the following conditions: He comes into the game with a lead of no more than three runs and pitches at least one full inning; he comes into the game with the potential tying or winning run on base, at bat, or on deck; he pitches effectively for at least three innings after entering the game.

set-up reliever A relief pitcher who is used immediately before the closer.

slide A slide occurs when a player drops to the ground when running toward a base in order to avoid being tagged out.

slider A pitch that is a combination of fastball and curveball—curving near the end of its flight.

stolen base When a runner successfully advances to the next base while the pitcher is delivering a pitch.

strike A pitch that is swung at and missed or a pitch that is in the strike zone and is not swung at. A foul ball counts as a strike unless it would be the third strike. Three strikes and the batter is out.

strike zone   The area directly over home plate up to the batter's chest (roughly where the batter's uniform lettering is) and down to the knees.

suicide squeeze   A squeeze play occurs when there is a runner on third base and fewer than two outs. The batter hits a bunt, expecting to be thrown out at first base but hoping the runner at third scores. In a suicide squeeze, the runner takes off for home before the pitch is thrown. If the batter does not bunt, then the runner is an easy out.

umpire   The official who rules on plays. For most baseball games, a home-plate umpire calls ball and strikes, and other umpires in the infield rule on outs at bases.

walk   A walk results when the pitcher throws four balls out of the strike zone and the batter does not swing at them. The batter is awarded first base. Also known as a base on balls.

walk-off home run   A game-ending home run by the home team—so named because the losing team has to walk off the field.

BIBLIOGRAPHY

The Associated Press. "Henderson Becomes Mets 1b Coach, Hojo Takes Over As Hitting Coach." ESPN.com, July 13, 2007. Available online at http://sports.espn.go.com/espn/wire?section=mlb&id=2935691.

Bauleke, Ann. *Rickey Henderson: Record Stealer.* Minneapolis, Minn.: Lerner Publishing Group, 1991.

DiComo, Anthony. "Notes: HoJo Serving as Hitting Coach." MLB.com, July 12, 2007. Available online at http://newyork .mets.mlb.com/news/article.jsp?ymd=20070712&content_ id=2083137&vkey=news_nym&fext=.jsp&c_id=nym.

Fimrite, Ron, Bill Mandel, and Bruce Jenkins. *Three Weeks in October: Three Weeks in the Life of the Bay Area, the 1989 World Series, and the Loma Prieta Earthquake.* San Francisco, Calif.: Woodford Publishing, 1990.

Gammons, Peter. "The New Mays: Rickey Henderson Has All the Tools, Wins Over A's Fans with Magic Flair." *Boston Globe.* August, 27, 1981.

Gammons, Peter. "Oh, What a Show!" *Sports Illustrated.* October 16, 1989.

Henderson, Rickey, and John Shea. *Off Base: Confessions of a Thief.* New York: HarperCollins Publishers Inc., 1992.

James, Bill. *The New Bill James Historical Baseball Abstract.* New York: Free Press, Revised Edition, 2003.

Litsky, Frank. "Henderson Heads to Newark for Path Back to Majors." *New York Times.* April 29, 2003.

Madden, Michael. "The Best in the Business." *Boston Globe,* October 29, 1989.

Manoloff, Dennis. "One on One with Rickey Henderson." *Baseball Digest,* February 2003.

Martin, Billy, and Phil Pepe. *BillyBall.* Garden City, N.Y.: Doubleday & Company, Inc. 1987.

Quinn, Ryan. "A's Unveil Rickey Henderson Field: Youth Ballpark's Namesake Throws Out Ceremonial First Pitch." MLB.com, August 11, 2006. Available online at http://mlb.mlb.com/news/article.jsp?ymd=20060811&content_id=1605025&vkey=news_oak&fext=.jsp&c_id=oak.

Shea, John. "Looking Beyond Usual Suspects for Managers." *San Francisco Chronicle.* October 8, 2006.

Shea, John, and John Hickey. *Magic by the Bay: How the Oakland Athletics and San Francisco Giants Captured the Baseball World.* Berkeley, Calif.: North Atlantic Books, 1990.

Weir, Tom. "Inside Rickey's World, He Marches to His Own Beat." *USA Today,* September 26, 2001.

VIDEOTAPE

Champions by the Bay: The 1989 Oakland Athletics & San Francisco Giants. Major League Baseball Productions, 1989.

Baseball – A Film by Ken Burns. PBS Home Video. 1994.

FURTHER READING

Anderson, Dave, Murray Chass, Robert Lipsyte, Buster Olney, and George Vecsey. *The New York Yankees Illustrated History.* New York: St. Martin's Press, 2002.

Bissinger, Buzz. *Three Nights in August: Strategy, Heartbreak, and Joy Inside the Mind of a Manager.* Boston: Houghton Mifflin, 2005

Dickey, Glenn, Vida Blue, and Joe Morgan. *Champions: The Story of the First Two Oakland Dynasties and the Building of the Third.* Chicago: Triumph Books, 2002.

James, Bill. *The New Bill James Historical Baseball Abstract.* New York: Free Press; Revised Edition, 2003.

Lewis, Michael. *Moneyball: The Art of Winning an Unfair Game.* New York: W.W. Norton & Company, Inc., 2003.

Leventhal, Josh. *The World Series: An Illustrated Encyclopedia of the Fall Classic.* New York: Black Dog & Leventhal Publishers, 2007.

Markusen, Bruce. *A Baseball Dynasty: Charlie Finley's Swingin' A's.* Haworth, N.J.: St. Johann Press, 2002.

Neyer, Rob. *Rob Neyer's Big Book of Baseball Lineups: A Complete Guide to the Best, Worst, and Most Memorable Players to Ever Grace the Major Leagues.* New York: Fireside, 2003.

Smith, Ron. *Heroes of the Hall: Baseball's Greatest Players.* New York: Sporting News, 2007.

Travers, Steven. *A's Essential: Everything You Need to Know to Be a Real Fan!* Chicago: Triumph Books, 2007.

Ward, Geoffrey C., and Ken Burns. *Baseball: An Illustrated History.* New York: Alfred A. Knopf, Inc., 1994.

WEB SITES

Baseball Almanac
http://www.baseball-almanac.com

Baseball Library
http://www.baseballlibrary.com

The Baseball Page
http://www.thebaseballpage.com

Baseball Reference
http://www.baseball-reference.com

National Baseball Hall of Fame and Museum
http://www.baseballhalloffame.org

The Official Site of Major League Baseball
http://mlb.mlb.com

The Official Site of the Oakland A's
http://oakland.athletics.mlb.com

The Personal Web Site of Lou Brock
http://www.loubrock.com

PICTURE CREDITS

COVER
MLB Photos via Getty Images

INDEX

ABOUT THE AUTHOR

GREG ROENSCH is a writer who lives in San Francisco, California. He has written many books for young adults, including biographies of Bruce Lee and Vince Lombardi and studies of the Lindbergh kidnapping case and capital punishment.